Moving Horizons – The Landscape Architecture of Kathryn Gustafson and Partners

Jane Amidon

Moving Horizons
The Landscape Architecture of Kathryn Gustafson and Partners

With a Contribution by Aaron Betsky

Birkhäuser – Publishers for Architecture
Basel · Berlin · Boston

Layout and cover design:
Peter Willberg, London

This book was also published in German (ISBN 3-7643-7051-3)
and French (3-7643-7161-7) editions.

A CIP catalogue record for this book is available from the
Library of Congress, Washington D.C., USA

Bibliographic information published by Die Deutsche Bibliothek
Die Deutsche Bibliothek lists this publication in the Deutsche
Nationalbibliografie; detailed bibliographic data is available in the
Internet at <http://dnb.ddb.de>.

© 2005 Birkhäuser – Publishers for Architecture,
P.O.Box 133, CH-4010 Basel, Switzerland
Part of Springer Science + Business Media
Printed on acid-free paper produced from chlorine-free pulp. TCF ∞

Printed in Germany
ISBN 3-7643-2425-2

9 8 7 6 5 4 3 2 1

www.birkhauser.ch

Contents

The Long and Winding Path
Kathryn Gustafson Re-Shapes Landscape Architecture
Aaron Betsky

It is not about flowers. It is not about emptiness. It is about shape. Kathryn Gustafson and her various collaborators on two continents bring landscape architecture back to its most basic act: that of shaping the land. That does not mean that she does not use plants and planting, nor that she ignores the sequencing of open space that is so essential to the success of the designed landscape. It is just that the plants never dominate, while the abstract volume is never left alone. In every design, there is a shape: a bulge, a curve, a splay, a rise or just a gate that defines the landscape as having a substance all its own. For Kathryn Gustafson, landscape is a physical material that she molds in order to reveal something about the place, add something new, and blend nature and invention into a seamless whole. In so doing, she allows stories about the land and our intervention in that base material on which we have erected our artifices to be revealed.

Gustafson's work would not be possible if it were not for the changed nature of landscape architecture, however. It is not just that she has invented a new way of treating the landscape, but that she has drawn on recent innovations in the discipline and has exploited the expanded field on which it operates. The sites and scales of the designed landscape have become vastly larger, but so have the situations in which clients deem it appropriate to ask landscape architects to operate. There is no limit to where this can lead: "If there's sky, it's mine," Gustafson is fond of saying.

While Gustafson's work does offer a particular and defined experience, it is never a *hortus conclusus* or even a bounded garden in any traditional sense. The traditional notion of landscape architecture restricts the operation of the designer to a defined and demarcated field, hemmed in by walls and fences. If there is a wider vista, that is, significantly, a "borrowed landscape," whether in the Japanese tradition of a sequence of scales moving from the miniature trees within the garden to the "real" trees beyond that, or in the English park tradition of agricultural land that is used to continue vistas. In the end, ownership and use patterns restrict the realm of landscape architecture.

By contrast, the more formal, Italian and French, tradition in landscape architecture remains resolutely enclosed within its own geometry. The aim there is to make a complete space that conforms to an abstract notion of order laid on the land with little or no regard for the particularities of place. Here the garden is an alternative to the real world, in which every plant or flower can have a particular significance, the climate itself is sometimes altered, and there are no direct references to the world beyond the pleasant outdoor realm. What both traditions have in common is their treatment of the garden or designed landscape as an isolated artefact. Even with the expansion of what had been a private pursuit interior to the realm of the wealthy owner of a palace or country retreat into public parks and open spaces in the late 18th and 19th centuries, the space of the designed landscape remained a defined and enclosed one. The walls around Central Park in New York and the London squares, but also the radical difference almost all designed exterior spaces enacted between their areas and their surroundings, continued the notion that landscape architecture makes an artificial fantasy interior with natural means. The fusion of many of the traditions of both romantic and rational design in modernist landscape architecture only reinforced this sense of controlled fantasy, replacing flowing forms with floating planes and rigid geometries with a collage aesthetic of overlapping fragments.

There are, of course, other traditions evident in landscape architecture, but they are ones that have been recognized only recently. Again, these can be divided roughly into two kinds, one of which sees the landscape as a more rational domain, while the other sees it as a romantic escape. However, both are tied in fundamental ways to that which is not visible in the landscape, but connects it to much larger physical and social structures. This secret history of landscape architecture would contrast the planning, building and expression of infrastructural elements with the discovery of existing landscapes as a form of landscape architecture. It is, in other words, the domain of engineers on the one hand, and the *flaneur*, voyager, vagabond or tourist on the other.

In the former tradition, the landscape comes into being as a designed entity by the intersection of a built extrusion of the artificial world of the city with what we can, perhaps only retroactively, call nature. The line of the aqueduct, the road, the canal or, later, the train tracks, the march of high tension electricity pylons and the engineering works that bring fresh water into the city and sewage out, all have a clear and sculptural form that does not so much create an environment as it allows us to measure, put into perspective and come to a clear relationship with what is otherwise just endless and undifferentiated land. Though these pieces were rarely designed to create a pleasing rhythm or appearance (at least until the early 19th century), they had an effect that can only be called aesthetic. By providing a point of perspective, a frame or a line of reference, they allowed nature to become a picture that could be enjoyed.

With the tearing down of city walls and defensive works, this infrastructure entered into the city, at times taking on the task of making space as well as providing a service. Such was certainly the case, for instance, in the integrated design of roads, canals, sewage systems and metropolitan railroad tracks in Vienna, under the direction of Otto Wagner and, twenty years later, in Chicago, at the instigation of Daniel Burnham.

Those public spaces that are not parks or squares, but roads or other linear interruptions of the city grid that also serve aims such as transportation, took on a quality that combined the heroic and no-nonsense scale of engineering projects with the tradition of differentiating public space so that it would be recognizable. In the 20th century, this engineering aesthetic reached its apotheosis in the non-urbanized landscape as the tendrils of the city took the shape of gigantic dams, levees, bridges and tunnels. Here, for the first time, infrastructure took on a consciously designed shape, a sculptural presence that provided a stock of symbolic imagery. Landscape architects and thinkers such as Ian McHarg then posited this as the discipline's central task.

One could equally well argue that it was not so much that infrastructure became more designed (though this certainly has been the case in an almost unbroken line leading towards more and more self-conscious design for the last two centuries), but that what we think of as a designed landscape has changed. Once artists and writers were confronted with the modern metropolis in the 19th century and once they, moreover, realized that it could not in the end be tamed, they began to find beauty exactly in its uncontrollable force, as well as in our heroic confrontation with its immeasurable scale. The fact that infrastructure was so ignorant of its effect on the land or the city, and offered an at times absurd alternative to the measured and comprehensible orders of the visual field, made it a sublime alternative.

We tend to think of such landscape forms as existing outside of the city, but the urban environment also took on sublime qualities, at least for artists. Soon it was exactly the messy, the dark and the huge that fascinated painters in Paris and writers in London. The train station sheds of which the Impressionists were so fond, the dark alleys where the life of the city happens in the works of Dickens and the Russian novelists, and the undetermined suburban realm where Henry James's or Theodore Dreiser's characters move offer quite literally different vistas. They are places where the land is formed by an almost incomprehensibly wide array of forces, many of them of a technological kind that are seen as beautiful exactly because they are so varied and beyond our understanding.

What is essential here is that it is only the narrative of exploration, the continuous experience of the viewer or reader, and the fragmentary nature of such spaces that makes them into what I would insist on calling a form of designed landscape. By describing what otherwise is not noticed, the artist turns what is as unformed as nature into a coherent environment with its own features and logic. The difference is that this realm is not isolated from the world around it, but embedded in it, appearing outside of the narrative only as isolated and meaningless fragments. The heroic and sculptural forces that had been posed in the landscape here dissolve into the city, leaving it to the user, if she or he is alert enough, to uncover that landscape through the markers it leaves behind.

This is not to say that such embedded or virtual landscapes exist only in the darkest reaches of the city. They are also the picturesque and linear worlds described by the green lines next to major roads on tourist maps, the vistas of the American West that shape the western or "oater," and the routes that describe a connection between places of either secular or religious tourism. Such virtual landscapes have deep roots in the worlds of vagabonds, travelers and pilgrims, who created a coherence not just in their tales, but also in marks on trees and heaps of stone along the road, but, as J. B. Jackson was fond of pointing out, it was not until mobility intersected with aesthetic appreciation in the middle-class culture of the 19th century that it really can be called a coherent, if often latent, landscape.

Lately, the continuous landscapes of the engineer and the vagabond have tended to approach each other in the design, for instance, of freeways that try to answer to both the call for efficiency and aesthetic pleasure (as in Lawrence Halprin's designs for the I-280 in California), but also in art-making practices that either document the most engineered landscape (think, for instance, of the photographs of Andreas Gursky or Richard Misrack), or that literally install themselves as lines in the landscape, as in the work of Christo and Jeanne-Claude, Robert Smithson or Richard Serra. This is where all the landscape traditions come together, as Rosalind Krauss pointed out thirty years ago: as artworks in the expanded field.

I would argue that Kathryn Gustafson, along with a few of her contemporaries in both the United States and Europe, has assimilated all four of these traditions (romantic and rational landscape design; engineered infrastructure and narrative exploration), as well as their confluence in certain forms of art, and transformed them back into a form of landscape design that defines itself as distinct and focused, but not isolated and compelling. It is landscape architecture as a way of making a space that makes us aware of the land and our shaping of it.

There is an important strain in Gustafson's work that is purely sculptural. This is most evident in her earliest large-scale work, such as the "Meeting Point" project in Morbras, of 1986, and her various landscapes for corporate clients such as Shell during that same period in France. In Morbras, the infrastructural intervention in the landscape (a new reservoir) becomes the opportunity for creating an undulating and sensual shape out of closely cropped grass-covered mounds. Bringing to mind the work landscape architects such as George Hargreaves were producing at the time, it also echoes in Gustafson's own work, as in the recent project for a highway entry into the city of Marseille. Here the work is almost completely abstract, and also closely aligned with the making of lines in the landscape. These lines become independent forms without removing themselves from the scene. At times, Gustafson even makes infrastructure itself, as she did in designing the bridge at the Costa Mesa shopping mall and in the EDF pylons for the French electricity company.

The opposite tendency in Gustafson's work is to create a narrative that flows through the existing landscape. Moments that are fragments of traditional garden and park typologies, such as herb gardens, fountains and shaped fields or *gazons*, are strung together along paths that both use and quite often accentuate topographical site differences. Here her works share a common language, to a certain extent, with those of Yves Brunier. The prototype within Gustafson's work for this approach is the elaborate park on a steep slope in Terrasson, France, which she called in the competition scheme, appropriately enough, "Fragments of the History of Gardens." The various elements of the park themselves have evocative names such as "Axis of the Wind" and "Ephemeral Tracings," as if Gustafson was trying to sing alive the mute earth through her arcs and mono-cultural beds placed between patches of dense forest. Here the designer's sculptural tendencies become literal and take the shape of elements such as a steel weather vane and a gold anodized aluminum loop cutting through the forest. These are also the least successful parts of the design, and seem somewhat jarring when they reappear in later work as well. It is as if Gustafson cannot satisfy herself with the making of a sculptural narrative with landscape, and instead uses elements that make that story explicit.

These independent works of art have another function, however, and that is to make the invisible apparent. Gustafson has long been fascinated by the unseen forces that shape our experience of place, and uses her weather vanes and other tracing devices to make these elements visible. She did this with particular success in the installation she created for the San Francisco Museum of Modern Art in 2001, as part of the "Revelatory Landscapes" exhibition. Here the usual path winding up the side of the hill led visitors to wind chimes and metal spinners that made them aware of the strong wind on the site. Sheltering chairs built out of the same material used to house drainage culverts let those visitors shelter from that strong force.

Gustafson keeps going back and forth between her undulating landforms and her winding, narrative paths, at times combining the two in one plan or tying them together with ennobled bits of infrastructure. She used the latter strategy in the elaborate 2003 design for the covered Marion Oliver McCaw Hall courtyard, where the architecture itself becomes a pergola-like grid and the lights of the stage inside are pulled outside and abstracted into environmental elements. The sculptural attitude towards the land, on the other hand, dominates but is also fragmented and turned into a collection of discreet landscape fragments in the Chicago Lurie Garden, part of the larger Millennium Park development of 2004. Here a large green hedge provides a frame that partially encloses the site and leads to a long boardwalk over an artificial body of water, which in turn is edged by a patchwork of different perennials Gustafson chose in collaboration with Piet Oudolf. There is a strong sense of a heroic, autonomous object made out of land, and yet the park also dissolves into a series of episodic fragments.

What ultimately ties the Chicago park together, and what forms the binding and focusing element in almost all of Gustafson's work, is water. It was there as the focus in Morbras, but it was also there in Terrasson, forming a continual line or "seam" that wound itself down the slope in counterpoint to the path, creating moments of encounter that were purely sensual, but also directly tied to the land and its needs, before turning into fountains that formed an autonomous element at the base of the park. When Gustafson uses water as infrastructure and narrative seam, as part of the scene and as independent (but ephemeral) object, her work has its strongest coherence.

Such is certainly the case in what is her finest achievement to date, the Diana, Princess of Wales Memorial Fountain in London, completed in 2004. Gustafson and Porter cleared out the English landscape park, abstracted it into her undulating and rhythmic grass mounds, and then intersected that sculptural base with an object that is itself a piece of infrastructure turned in on itself to become sculpture. The oval shape curves continually as it slides down the hill, taking the water with it and allowing that malleable material to take on a variety of different characteristics as it encounters various episodes, induced by a different treatment of the stone as well as by the hill's slope, along its journey to the adjacent lake. It is possible to read the Memorial as an evocation of the Princess's life, but one can also see it as a revelation of that fragment of the hilly British landscape, with its rills and creeks tending towards the Thames; a movement that is today only visible as a string of parks reaching north and west from London's old governmental core. Or one can see the Memorial as a completely abstract element that tells a story only about slope, water, shape and sequence, making one aware of the essential sensuality of all that we remake through our artifice.

Gustafson's work is not always this refined, and she does not always have the chance to make a work that is this laden with potential meaning and association, but she has a remarkable ability to exploit any given site for its sculptural and narrative potential. From the Westergasfabriek Culture Park, a public park on the site of a former gas works in Amsterdam, where from 1996 on she used a fragmentary excavation and preservation of the industrial heritage (the gas works themselves) to evoke the history of the site and focus the discreet episodes along the diagonal path seaming the sculptural lawn meant as seating area for audiences listening to outdoor concerts, to her recent designs for the Garden of Forgiveness in Beirut, where the Roman geometry of *cardo* and *decumanus* cut through a seemingly rigorous sequence of strips of planting that themselves are cut to reveal archaeological fragments, Gustafson is working around the world to uncover the hidden potential of any site. At the same time, she is, in projects such as the 2000 garden of the Rose Planetarium in New York, making some of the grandest and most self-confident pieces of land sculpture our culture has seen.

Gustafson is, of course, not alone in her exploration of infrastructure for its sculptural potential and the replacement of traditional and bounded gardens by episodic fragments along non-linear paths. Many other landscape architects are exploring similar themes, and to a large extent this is also because of the situation in which they find themselves. More and more they are asked to explore landscapes that are not a *tabula rasa*, and in which their task is to uncover what was there before as much as they have to invent something new – Duisburg Nord Landscape Park, by Peter Latz, is only the most famous example of a world-wide development. More and more they also have to make open spaces that contain not just places for relaxation and enjoyment, but are also integrated parts of the urban or ex-urban infrastructure: new sewage plants and artificial wetlands, rooftop gardens over newly built wings and roads make up a very large percentage of their work. But beyond these practical concerns, landscape architects also have come to realize that their work by its very nature exists at the intersection between infrastructure and exploration, rather than as a bounded domain, and are designing their work as such. Again, their reasons are pragmatic as much as they are aesthetic, as landscapes function as much as education and research and development for ecological concerns as they do as places of escape and leisure.

Gustafson's ability to tie together these two aspects of contemporary landscape architecture – the sculptural revealing and abstraction of the land and the experimental narrative formed of episodic collages of artificial elements of nature – and to conceive them as coming out of deeper structures – both literally, on the site, in the infrastructure, and metaphorically – makes her work so effective and so pleasant. Landscape architecture is indeed no longer just about flowers, nor is it about emptiness, but it is about opening up a space in which the artifice of our culture and its relationship to the land on which we have erected it can become evident to our eyes and our entire bodies, and we can go exploring this new hybrid space of human activity.

The Landscape Architecture of Kathryn Gustafson and Partners
Jane Amidon

I.

Bringing into being a book on one's work is an involved task. Much like designing and constructing a landscape, it entails entwined processes of critical assessment, creative production and extensive logistics. At what stage is it worth the effort to undertake such a commitment? Toward the beginning of a career, with hopes of gaining recognition and establishing a reputation? At the close, as a definitive record of achievement? Or perhaps somewhere in the middle is best, to document a life's work in progress. For Kathryn Gustafson, this publication makes sense right now, because if parallel efforts are peeled apart to be read independently of one another, the trajectories of her career are simultaneously embarking in new directions, entering into a confident midpoint, and gaining a sense of maturity.

Short of replicating oneself in triplicate, how is this upending of time's linear continuum – the primary arbiter of a career's evolution – possible? In this case, it has to do with dual operating modes of individual growth and professional development. After graduating from the Ecole Nationale Supérieure du Paysage in Versailles in 1979, Gustafson established a small design practice in Paris. Her first public commissions came as a result of transportation infrastructure programs generated by the French government. As principal of the firm and often working in association with landscape architect Sylvie Farges, Gustafson produced widely published landscapes such as the Morbras "Meeting Point" earth works (1986), Shell Headquarters (1991) and L'Oréal research facility (1992). When the economy of France changed and opportunities arose elsewhere, Gustafson exited the firm and partnered with Neil Porter to form the London-based Gustafson Porter office in 1997. Mary Bowman joined the partnership in 2002. In 2000 a second partnership, Gustafson Guthrie Nichol, opened in Seattle with partners Jennifer Guthrie and Shannon Nichol.

In terms of professional productivity, at the writing of this essay, landscapes implemented by Gustafson's first firm are mature and are a highly legible representation of early concerns. At the same time, important sites recently opened reveal new creative directions shaped by the collaborative tactics of Gustafson Porter (GP) and Gustafson Guthrie Nichol (GGN). Guided by a common set of design principles, the projects of each office develop in somewhat different directions depending on authorship, contributing voices and local/continental contexts.

Aside from evolving partnerships that have produced two distinct bodies of work (the mature and the emerging), Gustafson's personal growth as an artist and landscape architect can be considered to be at a midpoint. With a degree in fashion design, gained in 1972 from The Fashion Institute of Technology (New York) and a subsequent career change and diploma from Versailles in 1979, crucial periods of creative interaction with colleagues and mentors in the 1980s and 1990s deeply influenced Gustafson. The formative impact of working with the engineers Peter Rice and Henry Bardsley, architects Ian Ritchie and Bernard Tschumi, and sculptor Igor Mitoraj continues in recent projects with leading figures including Piet Oudolf, master plantsman, Robert Israel, theater set designer, and architects Peter Bohlin, Norman Foster, Renzo Piano, James Polshek and James Poulson.

In addition to these and other external influences, unavoidably a design persona is subjected to inner psychological filters. Call it intuition or emotional response, manifestations of subconscious impulse can be detected – although not necessarily explained – in everyone's work. The observation that Kathryn Gustafson currently occupies an intermediate and ongoing phase of personal productivity reflects the potential inherent in cross-fertilization of the internal (psyche) and the external (environment).

II.

To get at the roots of Kathryn Gustafson's work, we must speak about her personal background briefly, influential colleagues, current and historic works in allied fields (the artists, writers and architects from whom she derives inspiration), and tangentially, politics and economics. One cannot separate developments in the supposedly rational side of our culture – the economy, politics – from Gustafson's instinctive shaping of the land. While we note that her work is equal parts profound reaction to life events and the vicissitudes of national economies, we must also point out that which does not appear to be of great importance: the communal ideologies of contemporary place making, or put more simply, dominant cultural trends in landscape architecture. One could say that over the past two decades, Gustafson's work offers one of the more direct responses of inner dialog to client and site. She mediates between a private realm and public expression. In translating *parti*[1] into land form, water body, ground texture, light effect and spatial volume, Gustafson seems to eschew for the most part the profession's stylistic and theoretical discourse.

Not to make this point too broadly, as obviously most successful figures are to some degree well aware of what their contemporaries are doing. But rather, a finer point is being made here: Kathryn Gustafson greatly admires selected figures without being directly affected. She is more attuned to global dialogs of peace and war, environmental issues, women's rights and international political agendas. In some way, the field of landscape architecture is limited for her scope of artistic interest. Gustafson uses the medium of landscape – figured terrain, proactivated water and light – to produce commentaries that are site-specific and conceptually far-reaching. Some might argue that it is impossible to admire another's work without, on a subconscious level, using that work as a point of reference or departure. In Kathryn Gustafson's approach

there are glimpses or echoes of the familiar, but it is difficult to determine what is intentionally referential and what are merely coincidental mnemonics. Gustafson cites the work of French architect Claude Parent as an inspiration. Without being able to put a finger on specific effects, there is a correspondence between GP and GGN's prioritizing of the figural horizontal body and the architectural profession's current interest in organic topologies and uninterrupted volumes.

Given theorist Sanford Kwinter's talk of "matter is the new space,"[2] the muscular morphology of continuous surface and topographical mass found in numerous Gustafson projects – as well as the firms' sensitivity to how bodies move through and react to the materiality of a space – is a significant contribution to the canon of contemporary built works.

When asked to identify noteworthy voices in allied fields of design, art, and performance that offer parallels to her own interests, Gustafson mentions choreographer William Forsythe's attraction to the extremes of his medium. She admires the self-evidence of artist Richard Tuttle's works, and wonders what the music of Moby would look like as landscape. Sculptors Isamu Noguchi (also a landscape architect), Ellsworth Kelly and Richard Serra contributed to her understanding of form and space. Gustafson lists one of her favorite

This 50 × 40 centimeters bas relief plaster model was produced by Gustafson circa 1994 as part of a series of exploratory works in which the designer relayed emotional responses to external stimuli into sculptural form. In this piece, based on an animal hide stretched across a drum head, one sees evidence of Gustafson's early interest in effects of fullness and emptiness. Two sides roll inward to the main body with solid fluidity to create non-regular, continuous topographic mass.

designed landscapes in the United States as Dan Kiley's Henry Moore Sculpture Garden at the Nelson-Atkins Museum in Kansas City. The clarity of unfolding, ordered spaces as one moves between terraced planes is bold in her memory. However, the neoclassical language and controlled geometries are a far cry from Gustafson and partners' favored techniques. More explicitly akin to GP and GGN's approach are the landscapes of the French landscape architect Michel Desvigne, a contemporary of Gustafson and fellow Versailles graduate. There is an awareness of the body in the landscape espoused by Desvigne that rings true with Gustafson's dedication to "focusing people to feel the earth."

III.

The amenability of Gustafson's design approach to others who attended Versailles in the early years of its resurrection reflects the strength of pedagogical direction provided by Michel Corajoud, and before him, Jacques Sgard (the latter is regarded by Gustafson and others as the talent that forged the foundation for the current direction of contemporary landscape architecture in France). As described by Sébastien Marot and Manuel Delluc, beginning in 1973 the school "transformed into a true think tank in which an alternative point of view on design" took shape, demanding a refocus on the urban fringe, the rise of infrastructural decentralization and a "reading of the site itself."[3] Specifically, Corajoud taught his students about the power of phenomenology as opposed to landscape as decoration, and that "well before becoming the object of a design project, a landscape is the bearer of complex memory."[4] In her final year at Versailles, Gustafson apprenticed in Sgard's office, a position that exposed her to Sgard's abilities to read landscape and shape topographical surfaces. It is Sgard's work, in particular a land movement installation at the Parc Floral in Bois de Vincennes, that compelled her to enter into the profession of landscape architecture.

It is not difficult to find in Gustafson's approach a legacy of *in situ* anchoring, although originally the conceptual framing often was more abstract than concrete: the gentle billows of earth that trace the sun's movement across the Esso corporate headquarters grounds refer to "what is obscured and what comes to light," for example, as opposed to prioritizing artifacts of previous site incarnations. Topography, plantings and water are atavistic tools that call forth geologic, ecologic, social and urban histories but reject the didactic framing of a coherent narrative. In the newer projects of GGN, design elements are used to bring forth expressive site facts such as the Light and Dark Plates of the Lurie Garden (Chicago) and the use of illuminated glass at the Seattle Civic Center. Recent GP schemes sometimes respond less explicitly to literal context but with heightened rationality to the specific needs of site users, resulting in inventively functional, visually poetic solutions such as the contoured turf amphitheater at Swiss Cottage Open Space (London)

and the stone canyons and scree terraces of the National Botanic Garden of Wales. Although founded on the objective (past events), it is revelation of the subjective, sensory experience of place that remains the primary design effort of the two partnerships.

An assertive female from a close-knit family in the Yakima Valley of Washington State, Kathryn Gustafson entered Versailles as an older student, politically informed, ready to challenge and to be challenged. She carried knowledge of her own set of interests, a collection of painters, sculptors, musicians, photographers, dancers, athletes, writers that served (and continue to serve) as an inner sounding board and varied aesthetic resource. Much has been made of the possible carry-over of Gustafson's prior training in fashion design to the comfort she exhibits in molding land into non-regular topographies, but it is images of bodies in motion and their "arc of energy" that inform the tensing and relaxing of site contours more than translations of draped fabrics.

Designing a landscape by seeing the connection between body form and land form is a way to understand terrain by finding in site contours what one sees in the landscape of the body. The human body in motion through a site that itself has an internal skeleton and fleshed-out contours — body to body — drives most schemes. The body moves through a site as both a physical presence and an emotional being: perceptions are a mix of the intellectual and the sensorial.

Beyond the teachings of its instructors, Versailles' location contributed to Gustafson's love of manipulating the ground plane. "Versailles is my biggest influence, by far my favorite garden," she says. The grandeur of scale, the sense of discovery as one progresses through spatial sequences, the massive inclined planes seem to captivate the American as she returns to Le Nôtre's masterpiece at least twice a year. Often she brings a measuring tape, or counts steps to figure out a newly found moment, entering dimensions into a Palm Pilot

A private residential project in Paris, Gold Wall (1990) sits over sub grade parking on a thirty by fifteen-meters urban lot. Dimensioned in accordance with the Golden Mean, the concrete wall is extravagant in its gold leaf surfacing but utilitarian in its screening of stairwell and ventilation. With minimalist jargon the scheme responds to the client's wish for a contemporary private garden while providing Gustafson an opportunity to synthesize reading of site and context with internally driven dialectics.

amid the 18th-century *tapis*. "The geometry orients you, but you're always pulled to proceed, to move into the next piece," she describes. One wonders if there is a landscape architect alive immune to Le Nôtre's power. Some are convinced his placement of vertical elements to create spatial volume with green architecture is timeless. Others find his strong articulation of the horizontal plane to be essential. What binds the various perceptual strengths of the royal garden? Scale. What attracts Kathryn Gustafson? Scale. Yet to walk in a site designed by Gustafson, there's no sense of Le Nôtre lurking in the shadows. It is, possibly, shades of the Picturesque one detects if observing closely.

Over the past few years, Gustafson admits, gardens of the Picturesque have entered her sphere of interest. It is about the sense of pulling eye and foot through a site, but in an abrupt break from Cartesian planar space, the Picturesque contorts its relationship with the horizon. In project research conducted for the renovation of the Crystal Palace grounds in London, Neil Porter phrases GP's intentions (based on interpretation of Joseph Paxton's Victorian festival grounds) as "the evolution of space, a non-constant that spans, stretches, stops, rolls." Placing aside the thirst for reform and transcendent visions of idealized nature that helped fuel the growth of the picturesque movement in the age of the Industrial Revolution, it is the spacial discovery derived from constructed land forms and modulated horizons to which Gustafson (and her partners to varying degrees) responds.

Outside the manipulation of scale and horizon, Gustafson has devoted a fair amount of energy, both in solo works and with partners, to developing plant palettes that provide a layer of meaning or site/context-specific meaning. Information is incorporated that references plant schemas of previous eras (for projects such as the genealogical gardens in Boston's North End Parks), alternate ecologies (post-industrial sites such as the Cultuurpark Westergasfabriek in Amsterdam), client practices (as at the L'Oréal corporate garden outside of Paris) or regional identity (the Garden of Forgiveness in Beirut).

While Gustafson's early commissions were designed for limited public exposure, increasingly the work of GP and GGN is in the spotlight of intensely urban locations. In working with these types of projects, Gustafson and partners acknowledge the strategic influence of historic models, but the thinking is uniquely contemporary. Empty formalism (the downside of neo-classicism, modernism and process-based post-modernism in the landscape), stagnant nostalgia (the picturesque as categorized by some current-day critics), environmental prerogatives (at the risk of design-less design), borrowed art theory, and systems-based matrices offered by some landscape architects, architects, urbanists (as yet not fully reality-checked for biological or social success) are all present in the work of leading landscape architects today; one would be hard pressed to associate Gustafson's early work or the output of the current partnerships with any of these approaches.

Gustafson cites one contemporary park as having an influence on her approach to innovative public space making. In the mid-1980s, the La Villette competition positioned itself as a venue for the establishment of a new 21st-century park typology. In the early stages of her career, a decade out of graduate school, Gustafson was selected to work on one of the small garden commissions within the park as well as to do a study of Bernard Tschumi's overall scheme. Conceived in reference to Kandinsky's study of point, line and plane, Tschumi's plan represents a collection and collision of fragments from the surrounding urban environment. These forces generate their own energy to bind the city within the cohesion of the greater cultural landscape. In Gustafson's opinion the scheme succeeds because it is uncompromisingly a product of the time and mores that created it. La Villette is based on a concept of the urban culturescape. Parks before it were founded on models of nature, whether pastoral ideal or productive resource (located within the city, they were not of the city). Although outside the interpretation of Kandinsky's influential work and notwithstanding the necessity of the scheme's readability under public scrutiny, Gustafson believes it would have been interesting to bring La Villette's theoretically stringent two-dimensional *parti* fully into three dimensions. The planes, in particular, might be thickened or manipulated to create a stronger sense of space and discovery as one moves into the park. The result would be volumetric definition via a figural ground plane. In conversations with Tschumi and with the many contacts she made throughout the Villette project (including meeting Neil Porter in 1984), Kathryn Gustafson participated for a time in the theoretical discourse of contemporary park design but did not stray far from her inner dialog in terms of working method and design philosophy.

Central to Gustafson Porter's scheme for the Cultuurpark Westergasfabriek in Amsterdam (2004) is a shift from industrial operations to new cultural and environmental prerogatives. The site is engineered in a manner that speaks to the Netherland's history of water control and landscape reclamation while providing flexible spaces for both public agenda and individual exploration. Layers of factory history, polder ecologies and new uses network within a circuit of programmed pieces including the Color Field, Market Square, Cité des Artistes, Gas Holder Aquatic Ponds, Events Lake and Wet Gardens. Elongated vistas of woodland, water and field enlarge the scale of space within subtle horizon shifts of large land and water form.

IV.

"Why create something if not for people to interact with it?" with this question posed recently by Kathryn Gustafson, the discussion turns to six strands that weave through the partnerships' creative method. These strands give the design process an independent stance, and subsequently, determine its impact on the public. They include: the role of creative, critical site analysis; scale, the horizon and discovery; site as contextualized body; distillation of sensory experience; non-directive narrative; innovation in representation, construction and site solutions. Although these strands are easily found in the collaborative output of GP and GGN, they originated with Gustafson's earliest projects. Gustafson describes the evolution of her design process over time as a series of ladders and plateaus. She enters one plateau, full of things to investigate. Once questions are resolved to a certain degree, another ladder becomes evident. She begins to climb not knowing where ladders lead to. These days, the partners take ideas into different realms, developing trajectories in new directions that enable the practices to evolve beyond the instincts of a solitary designer. Operating within this open-ended scenario, the six process strands provide a consistent set of design values that now serve as a common language for the investigations of the independent London-and Seattle-based practices.

The role of creative, critical site analysis

As pointed out by Marot and Delluc in their appraisal of the initial phase of rebirth of the Ecole Nationale Supérieure du Paysage in Versailles in the 1970s, the landscape design pedagogy offered by Michel Corajoud and others, most likely that to which Kathryn Gustafson was widely exposed, took as its point of departure "not the proposed building project so much as a reading of the site itself, an examination of the possibilities… It also had a strong critical component."[5] This idea of site investigation embodying a critical dimension is essential to Gustafson's approach. Each project contains a conceptual armature that springs from Gustafson's (and later, her partners') assessment of site issues layered with an application of personal – sometimes political – interpretation. Typically, this final layer is not made public. Clients are well versed in a project's take on site history or contextual references, but may not be fully aware of the embedded meaning certain site elements hold for Gustafson or other team members. In a strange way, this ensures ultimate authenticity: you as the designer are the final audience and critic.

Another dimension of site analysis that places emphasis on the fusion of the creative and the critical is Gustafson's well-practiced technique of translating between site/context information and design *parti*. The leap from the rational (site data) to the intuitive (design gesture) is quite difficult for many to make. In Gustafson's practice (both solo and in partnerships), the leap happens early with small-scale grading sketches

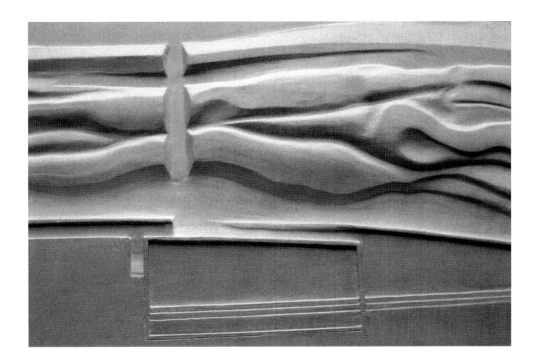

that inform large clay models of sculpted ground planes. According to Gustafson, analytical information is absorbed but, she says, "I don't think in a linear manner." She literally "feels" the design emerge as vivid land form from the clay and in sketches. This may in part explain why, as discussed later in this essay, only recently within GP and GGN has responsibility for each project's first model been expanded beyond Gustafson to other partners. It may be that it takes a decade or more to gain the ability to turn off the analytical brain, to find resonant terrain between eye, hand and clay.

Scale, the horizon and discovery

Scale is the quality most discussed in Gustafson's work. Yet it is also one of the more difficult to pin down, to intellectualize. One suspects this is because – as at Le Nôtre's great gardens or in the undulating folds of Capability Brown's estates – scale is determined to a significant degree by visual contact with a shifting horizon while one's feet are firmly connected to the ground. It is nearly useless to describe verbally how the shaping of form and horizon line effect perception of place. This is particularly true of Gustafson's urban works, where non-regular molding of the ground plane is startlingly vocal amidst the mostly orthogonal volumes and measured parts that control and orient. In opposition to the "knowing" of regular organizations, Gustafson and partners seek to give people a sense of discovery.

"There is a line through all of the work: manipulation of perceptual space," says Gustafson. The schemes are about how people are guided by what they see and what they touch along the way: ground form and texture, plantings, water and light. Sites must be engaged to be known. Non-regular resolution of form encourages certain perspectives. But one certainly can identify the influence of classic structure also, albeit

The Passy scheme (a competition proposal, 1998, not built) offers a solution for social housing and 1.5 hectare of open space on steep terrain near the Passy Metro in Paris. Terraced gardens begin with a paved belvedere and descend sequentially through dense woodland and sculpted land, water feature and play area to a clean, linear space. The site invites movement to explore a dialog between the monolithic and the decorative, paralleling the neighborhood's architectural evolution through Art Nouveau into modernism. Gustafson collaborated on this proposal with architects Francis Soler and Bertrand Bonnier.

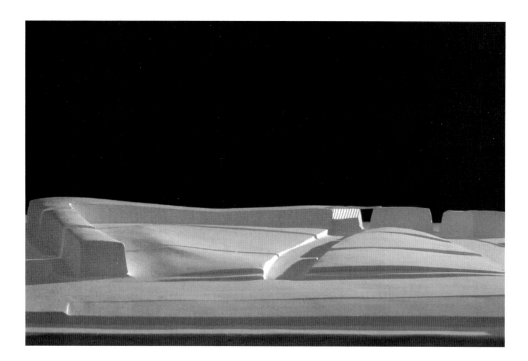

used sparingly: site lines that end on framed voids, a fascination with locating the body within space. "I want to guide views," the designer states, "by playing with scale and perspective, we can emphasize the relation of a body to an experience of place."

Site as contextualized body

It helps to use a medium of representation appropriate to design intent. For Gustafson, clay (cast into plaster) is ideal: monochromatic models allow designers and clients to understand pure form giving and making. At the core is the idea of muscled terrain, of contours swelling, cinching, ascending, breathing – in short, occupying space to the extent that ground plane becomes figure. "We are relating to a bigger kind of land-based sculpting," says Shannon Nichol. "We design a site as one body, solidly, all the way through." This method is an interpretive act that links a site's embodiment to its context, distinct history and conceptual underpinnings. It represents to some degree a collapsing of the middle ground so important to pictorial space. One occupies the material presence of the fore*ground* and by extension of a warping, continuous surface, the figured distant ground simultaneously. No threshold exists between the two conditions, they coexist and continually shift as one moves through the site and the relationship to various horizon lines changes.

Importantly, in Gustafson's work and increasingly in the schemes of other partners, horizontal continuity is a governing factor. Space is influenced by the placement of vertical objects, certainly, but it is the configuration of (modified) planes of earth that defines spatial volume. Never predetermined, undisputedly intuitive, horizontal modulation speaks with the gravity of geology in its bold simplicity. Constructed sites give the impression of having existed long before the project at hand. In a 1999 interview, critic Paula Deitz

A monochromatic model of the Lurie Garden (Chicago, 2004) reveals the essential naked figure. The thickened, sculpted ground and vegetal elements for a Light Plate and a Dark Plate are two aspects of the designers' interpretation of site history. Movement through the garden can occur efficiently along broad walkways or via varied and haptic engagement with the ground plane. Molded horizon lines define perception of scale depending on the viewer's location.

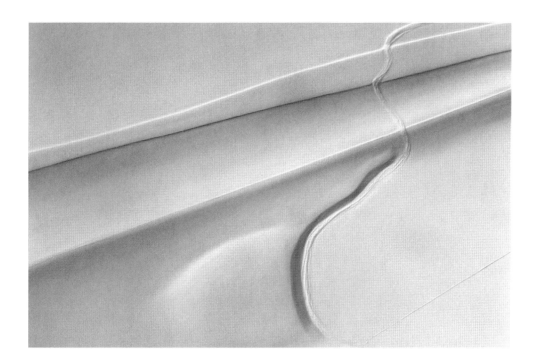

described Gustafson's approach in this way: "... landscape as an immense canvas to shape and manipulate."[6] One can sympathize with this view, as long as the canvas is agreed to be at the regional or global scale; Gustafson and her partners' methods should not be confused with a straightforward sculpting of land form that sits politely within site boundaries, beginning and ending neatly at the property line. Although just a handful of projects in the firms' joint histories develop site solutions without reshaping an entire area, the partners emphasize that this is due more to the type of commissions received than to a signature strategy of sculpting earth. Ground plane movement happens for a reason in disrupted sites. For projects with healthy existing surface conditions (often a balance of manmade and natural parts), water, paving, plantings and lighting are primary design tools. That said, however, Neil Porter points out that, "The fact that we liberate ourselves from the need to retain existing landforms, rather than see them as a barrier to change, is in a way a signature strategy – a strategy that creates the freedom to do the right thing for a site's context and clients' needs."

Distillation of sensory experience

The experience of discovery so critical to Gustafson's intentions is achieved often with horizontal manipulations, but also with sophisticated fusions of water and illumination effects. The dualities that succinctly describe Gustafson and subsequently GP's and GGN's work usually depend on heightened effects of light and water: "complex simplicity," "force and fragility," rational intuition," "feminine minimalism." An additional condition, "empty when full, full when empty" is in particular shaped by ambient ingredients. A number of projects such as the Square of Human Rights (Evry), the Government Offices Courtyards

A second 50 × 40 centimeters bas relief plaster model from Gustafson's mid-1990s sculpture series affirmed that the designer needed to build landscapes – it was not enough to work at the object scale. This piece, an exploration about the pathways of people, translates an inner emotional passage into topologies of force and fragility that intersect but do not affect one another. The measured simplicity of formal gestures establishes a resonant horizontality and expanded sense of scale.

(London), Ross Terrace (New York), and Seattle's Marion Oliver McCaw Hall and Civic Center depend on orchestrations of phenomena to orient users. At times with few occupants, thin sheets of water fill or flow over shallow indentations, or narrow water jets spring from paved surfaces. When gatherings occur, water is emptied for optimal plaza availability. Similarly, mesh, stone or glass scrims undistinguished by day glow as planes of light that enliven the pedestrian experience and change site experience. Distilled sensations give sites a degree of spatial complexity without additional physical elements. Ephemeral effects deepen relationships between materials, as the moods of stone, vegetation, and other surfaces alter depending on exposure. The interest, in one partner's phrasing, is in enabling "conscious perception."

In other projects, natural forces are harnessed to create site-specific sensory experience. The Wind and Sound Garden in Lausanne and the San Francisco MoMA installation featured devices that captured and amplified the wind's movement. At Esso, undulations in the ground plane measure passage of the sun. Initially a design tactic rooted in the study and revelation of site phenomena, in collaboration with her partners Gustafson's interest in sensory experience has narrowed its focus to more performative functions (such as the presence and absence of light and water indicating varying types of usage in public spaces – as opposed to more purely experiential investigations, such as breezes activating wind chimes). In plan, a scheme's structural logic may not be readily apparent; one gains understanding intuitively via experience of figural relationships and ephemeral effects. Scales of focus telescope and contract: sometimes it is about movement and perception of non-constant horizon lines, other times about discovery of a particular stone texture, leaf color, water pattern or shadow cast. Ideally, the designers say, visitors need to return to a landscape numerous times to fully grasp conceptual, spatial and material intentions. "It's about how you move, what your eyes rest on, what the depth of feel is, what you walk through, what you sit on," explains Gustafson.

Non-directive narrative

In Gustafson and partners' approach, big concepts (multi-layered) share importance with fine details. This in and of itself is not ground-breaking. But unique perhaps to the work is the wide array of resources drawn upon, synthesized and expressed in powerful landscapes. Site history, scientific data, international issues, private concerns, client factors, encounters with specific artists, research into materials – all of these simultaneously inform the partnerships' construction of meaning. It is the work of translation, and consistently imagination is valued over linear narrative. One won't gain quantifiable knowledge of time, place or context by visiting a Gustafson project, there is rarely a prescribed route to follow. Rather, the visitor is left with an impression of place, a memory of experiential qualities that link intuitively to larger issues. This kind of design requires to varying degrees an engineer's rationality, a philosopher's insight and an artist's impulse. It may be that the designer's personal motivations differ from the public version of the site story, leading to a truly flexible, idiomatic identity of place. When the question is posed, "What does it mean?" the answer must be generated by individual assessment instead of a static narrative.

Innovation in representation, construction and site solutions

In a quest for design integrity, Gustafson is not afraid to question her own methods: "How do you do contemporary that isn't sterile?" The offices try not to use any standard details; each condition is viewed as an opportunity for invention. From the early use of sanded, monochromatic plaster models as the means to communicate form giving and form making to the custom design of site furnishings for numerous projects, Gustafson and partners strive for coherency from design concept through representation and construction. As is true for most current-day design firms, digital collage and modeling greatly expands GP and GGN's abilities to portray spatial relationships, textures and colors. For the Diana, Princess of Wales Memorial Fountain, GP worked with technical consultants to scan the original hand-molded model and convert the data into digital files. The data was used by a quarry in Northern Ireland to cut the stone for the fountain's water channel. In some cases innovation springs not from new capabilities and tools but from careful reconsideration of site issues: when design intent and strict codes clash, such as at the Seattle Civic Center terraces, adjustments (in this case, of the section and realigned plant masses) serve both causes.

V.

The process strands described in the preceding section are deeply rooted in personal philosophies that continue to evolve through Gustafson's close collaboration with partners Neil Porter, Mary Bowman, Jennifer Guthrie and Shannon Nichol. In less than two decades, Gustafson's solo practice grew from designing remote highway interchanges and private, corporate commissions to giving life – now with the partnerships – to society's most symbolic and contested public sites. The relatively small London and Seattle offices are producing landscapes for leading institutional clients at a rate that is rare in the profession. In considering the impact of the six critical strands on the design methodology of the partnerships, it is useful to discuss the formation of Gustafson Porter (GP) and Gustafson Guthrie Nichol (GGN) in more detail.

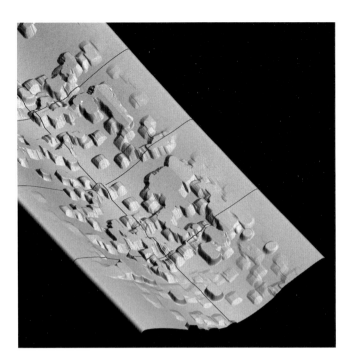 

Of the current partners, Gustafson and Porter have the longest history of collaboration. The two first worked together on the Parc de la Villette, Porter as an architect with the office of Bernard Tschumi and Gustafson on commission from the director of the park to design (with Ian Ritchie of RFR) interior schemes for the glass houses of the Museum of Science, Technology and Industry façade. With a diploma from the Architectural Association in London, Neil Porter taught at the AA and gained extensive experience in firms that include Alsop & Lyall, Ian Ritchie, Terry Farrell and John Lyall Architects (London) before partnering to direct GP in 1997. A background in architectural projects, he believes, is not so different from issues faced in GP's practice. When asked about his take on the dialog between landscape and architecture, Porter responds, "We take information around us, given to us or that we find for ourselves. We work with thoughts that then turn into spaces that people use. It is just as appropriate to landscape as it is to the way we may have thought about buildings or structures within buildings or pieces of furniture in a room." Also an architect now practicing a type of landscape architecture, Mary Bowman joined GP in 2002. Bowman is an American who studied at the Architectural Association after gaining an undergraduate degree at the University of Virginia. She worked at Foster and Partners for a decade and was a director at Walters and Cohen (London) before accepting Porter's invitation to join GP's growing practice. "I instinctively felt very comfortable with the work of GP and understood its language," says Bowman. "Neil and Kathryn's abilities to work simultaneously, intuitively and with an incredible degree of discipline, energizes the design process." In the London office, Porter and Bowman head up a steadily expanding staff whose numbers are currently at twenty and are roughly split between landscape architects and architects. "In our office there is an overlap between landscape and architectural form without boundary, which in its own way is very urban," says Bowman. Key support figures in GP include Sibylla Hartel and Max Norman. The interdisciplinary team allows the practice

This pair of images speaks about the power of precision when crafting specific effects of light, sound and water in the landscape. On the left is a computer generated model of a water channel floor segment of the Diana, Princess of Wales Memorial (London, 2004, digital modelling by Barron Gould-Texxus). On the right is a photograph of water bubbling up between submerged, illuminated glass panels at the Seattle Civic Center Hall of Justice (Seattle, 2004). Although minute in immediate scope, collectively the sensory stimuli – generated by creative technologies – build atmospheric qualities that feed into a site's narrative and influence spatial perception.

to move with technical fluency between diverse issues such as site contamination, building design and preservation of archaeological remains within the context of designed landscapes.

In Seattle Jennifer Guthrie and Shannon Nichol direct a current staff of fifteen. "For every project we do an incredible amount of research," explains Guthrie. "We find out how the place happened and then figure out how to connect people to that. We try to capture the soul of a place or a component of a region, to tie it back into its greater community." Meeting originally as colleagues at a Seattle-based design firm, Guthrie and Nichol partnered with Gustafson in 2000 after working together on several projects. Guthrie holds degrees in landscape architecture and architecture from the University of Washington. She brings to GGN projects interests that range from schematic design development through construction documentation and project management. Also a graduate of Washington's landscape architecture program, Nichol's work combines research with first-hand impressions of site and context; designs are intuitively worked out but factually founded in response to local history, geography and social factors. "My impulse for design is from an interest in the real," says Nichol. "We try not to do anything with the land that doesn't come from an inventive, thoughtful reaction. We try to respect that landscape is part of something bigger than anything you put on top of it or affix to it. It's not a building or a piece of art, it is land." GGN has recently recommitted to keeping the design dialog, once out of preliminary stages, open to the entire office. Group critique sessions keep the design intent on track and inspire new ideas over time with a simple, integrated system of checks and balances: design development and construction detailing are frequently compared to the original scheme to ensure coherency. Leading staff members tend to direct specific efforts across a breadth of projects, including Marcia West with expertise in construction management and ecological restoration, and Gareth Loveridge and Rodrigo Abela as design associates. Like GP, GGN is a mix of people trained in landscape architecture and/or architecture, some with additional degrees in engineering, geography, ecology and atmospheric sciences.

Within the partnerships, design begins as a reaction to information. One partner typically handles the conceptual transition between site analysis and site shaping, a process that varies considerably depending on who is at the helm. Given the geographic distance between offices and the number of projects in development, for the sake of efficiency and partner sanity it is necessary to share responsibility for schematic development and representation to the greatest extent possible. Lists of key words, gestural sketches and digital collage with photographs of texture samples are used to communicate initial ideas to partners, staff and clients. In both offices, the decisive expression of the preliminary design *parti* often occurs with the making of a large-scale plaster model. At one time Gustafson, in a hold-over from solo practice and as a testament to her sculpting skills, would isolate herself in a private studio for several days to work out cut/fill calculations, determine key contextual issues and produce a clay maquette (the clay model serves as a base from which a rubber die is formed to produce subsequent plaster casts). Increasingly, a partner in charge of a given project works on the clay maquette with frequent reviews with team members. Although tales are told that in the past Gustafson's brusque communications style and lofty expectations yielded an experience for younger team members known as "Kathryn 101," there exists a widely shared sentiment that Gustafson is a superb teacher and challenging partner who insists that others develop their ideas with intuitive and intellectual confidence.

It is likely that the personality quirks and communication abilities of each partner and team member relate to Gustafson in unique ways. In other words, in her leadership role Gustafson is not a constant. She flexes depending on the qualities of those around her. "Kathryn feels the design through landscape and I feel it through architecture; we start venting and creating with a mix of lucid and emotional stuff that we're both comfortable with," describes Porter. While an observer might guess that Gustafson's constant travel between offices and to sites across the globe would interfere with project schedules, the partnerships (particularly London, as Gustafson's home base is in Seattle) are accustomed to periods of absence interspersed with days of intense interaction. When she arrives, partners describe, it's possible to see Gustafson and hear her with fresh insight that isn't available to those who work with one another every day. In fact, it's the continual readjustments – the abruptness of contact – that give the partnerships precious clarity.

VI.

Why is the vision of the two partnerships increasingly sought by powerful arbiters of culture and what type of work is produced to satisfy the hunger for landscapes of lasting impact? There is a recognizable feel to Gustafson Porter and Gustafson Guthrie Nichol designs that offers simplicity without loss of conceptual rigor, clarity without severity. Land is not treated to an applied stylistic mask, schemes are generated by a desire
to communicate specific site sensations and forces of movement. Fluid horizontality – the thickened ground plane as a non-regular, continuous surface that is perceived somewhere between the organic and the artificial – often effects perception of scale and place. There is an interest in the real that skews toward a site's inheritance over pure abstractions. Finally, Gustafson and partners are advocates of the city, and rather than disguise the urban condition their work magnifies prosaic ingredients with modulating effects of elevation, illumination and inundation.

Although carrying evidence of independent processes, the products of the partnerships present a cogent body of work that can be organized into the following five categories: Visual Land, Encountering Land, Light and Water, Framed Space and Places of Translation. These categories, used as a framework to divide the book into five chapters, offer a means to understand how each project and its complex simplicity relate to the larger œuvre of Gustafson's early designs and the current success of Gustafson Porter and Gustafson Guthrie Nichol.

Visual Land:

Un-peopled spaces characterized by large land movement and elements operating at scales and grains beyond the site boundaries.

Encountering Land:

Forms of robust, graceful structure and fluid minimalism that engage the eye and foot in discovery.

Light and Water:

Effects that in their presence and absence qualify spatial perception and amplify material qualities, causing connection to a landscape via the senses.

Framed Space:

Interior or open spaces with an internally defined structure, often in association with a specific architectural frame.

Places of Translation:

Sites that embody interpretation of cultural contexts and environmental factors into contemporary landscape expression.

---

1 Author's note: as used here the term *parti* refers to the general organizational strategy of a design.

2 Sanford Kwinter at "The Shape of Things to Come" conference, January 17, 2004, Knowlton School of Architecture at the Wexner Center, The Ohio State University.

3 Marot, Sébastien, "Return of the Landscape," *Desvigne + Dalnoky: Return of the Landscape.* New York: Whitney Library of Design, 1997, page 7.

4 Delluc, Manuel, "Michel Desvigne and Christine Dalnoky," *ibid.* page 11.
5 Marot, *ibid.*
6 Deitz, Paula, "A Twinkling Terrace That Reaches for the Stars," *New York Times*, January 7, 1999.

Visual Land

Retention Basin and Park, Morbras

As Kathryn Gustafson's first major solo project, the "Meeting Point" project at Morbras demonstrates strategies that in retrospect have become fundamental to her design process. Morbras is a "visual land," a shaping of earth into formal forces. Morbras is important to landscape architecture and to the establishment of Gustafson's practice because it speaks with the scalar power of horizontal mass. The intuitive, reductive language of terrain and water at this scale – 300,000 cubic meters of earth were used – is more likely to be associated with civil engineering and earth artists. Familiar to garden makers of earlier centuries, in the 1980s, the technique was just beginning to resurface as a critical component of contemporary landscape architecture.

In 1984, five years after receiving her degree from Versailles, Gustafson was contacted by a municipal organization in the Seine and Marne region outside of Paris. With an emerging reputation for designing

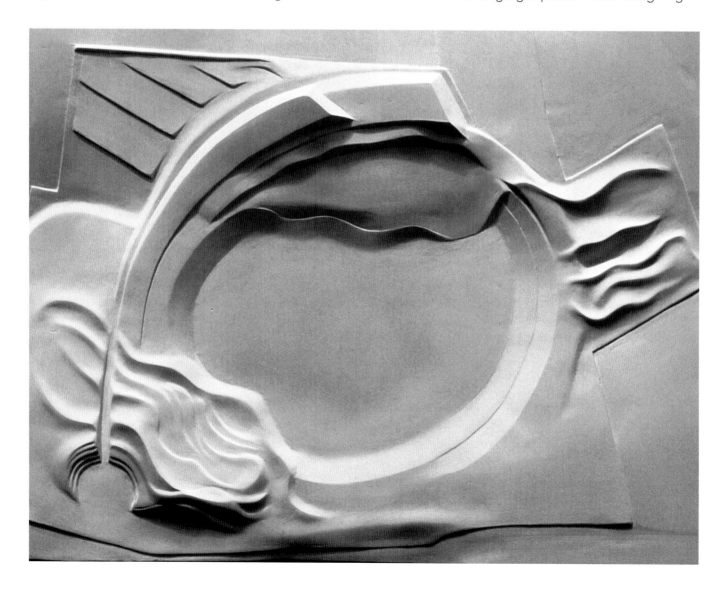

Explored primarily in clay, a grid of pins was pushed into the model's finished surface to determine spot elevations five meters on center for the grading plan. A second reference grid outlined each land form, marking the points from top to bottom of each slope. Sections were cut every five meters and placed onto the reference grid. Gustafson cast a fiberglass model for the small blade operator to understand the design in three dimensions – particularly, that the sculpted terrain needed to emerge and return fluidly to surrounding land to retain topographical integrity. When the park opened, "Meeting Point" presented stark, sinuous horizontality that matured over time with vegetation management.

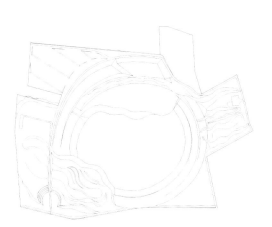

land works modeled in clay, the designer was hired to create a land form scheme with spoils excavated from a retention pond alongside the regional highway (to avoid the cost of soil removal). Gustafson approached the problem as an interpretation of site forces in order to translate the straightforward program into sculpted land that encompasses recreational lands, a picnic area, amphitheater, camping terraces and wetland fragments.

The scheme is an allegory of movements meeting in space. Two angular mounds form the thrust of the Strong force and hold the north side of the basin within a ramped ridge. The Fluid spills over the

Strong, inattentive and independent. An Insidious presence pushes at the arced edge, causing the Strong to adjust incrementally. A Maternal force embodies the totality of the composition

with an elliptical embrace that flattens in several areas to allow movement in and out. Parasitic elements feed off of the Maternal primary forces. Recreational program carved from or overlaid onto the

site forces include an amphi-theater and campsite shelves. Along the pre-existing river, new dells of the Parasitic planted with reeds filter agricultural run-off for swimming.

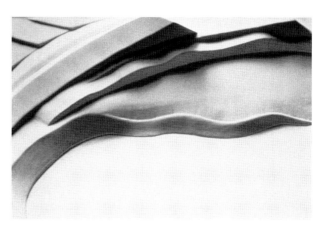

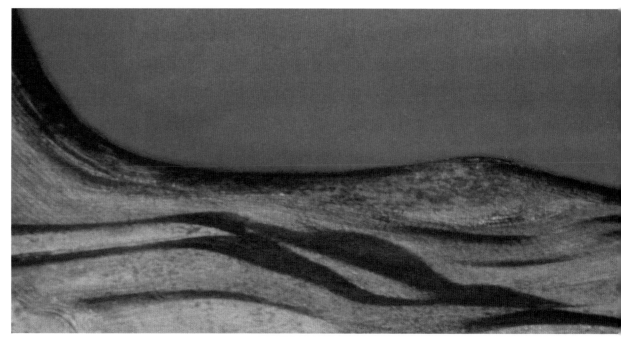

"Breast Plate" Tunnel Entrance, near Paris

In 1970, Cofiroute first proposed a connection between Rueil-Malmaison and the A13 in the densely populated suburbs of Paris. It wasn't until 1992 that the project was approved, primarily due to new tunnel-boring technology (a similar machine was used to build the Chunnel beneath the English Channel). Kathryn Gustafson was contracted to conduct site analysis and to propose a design solution for the tunnel entrance. Although not built, Breast Plate remains important to the trajectory of Gustafson's early design work.

The tunnel entrance cuts 16 meters into the earth. Terraced slopes receive this void as they ascend in a tight horseshoe from the tunnel grade. Moving outward, the terraces flatten into broad bands that meet the scale of the regional landscape. Four planting palettes distinguish four conditions: highest slopes, intermediate slopes, roadside zones and the classically-inspired tunnel entrance. The site's tiered profile

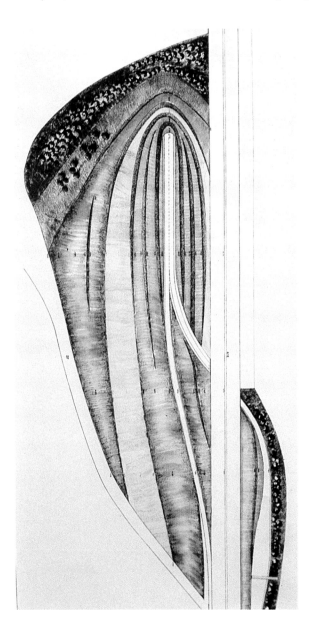
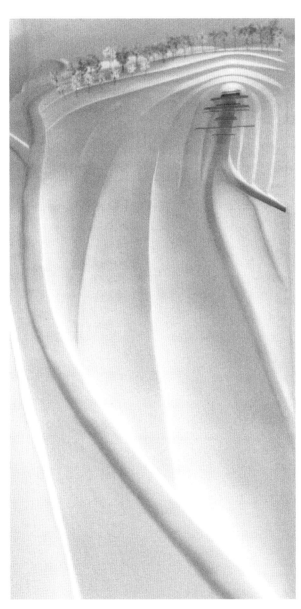

Gustafson's critical practice of form making in clay model and plaster cast successfully communicated her vision of the tunnel entry as a regionally scaled land sculpture. Sited in a protected agricultural valley famous for its beauty, the tunnel entry scheme included naturalized grasses on the highest slopes to create a textural transition to the surrounding wheat fields. Intermediate slopes contained ornamental grasses planted in linear swaths parallel to the roadway. Zones closest to the road edge held a prairie palette intended to be trimmed once per month for driving safety and to maintain a cultivated character. Above the tunnel entrance, fruit trees representing local farms segue to forest.

and color-coded grasses heighten the perception of entering a tunnel at high speed. Drivers register the experience of motion more acutely and gain a sense – primarily subliminally – of how the highway infrastructure sits within surrounding terrain. A series of metal bars bridge the tunnel entrance, stitching the loss of rendered earth and guiding the transition from protection/darkness to release/exposure.

The first pylon prototype was installed in the Rhone Valley in 2002. Constructed of galvanized, painted steel, the primary vertical of the pylons stands at an average of 50 meters/165 feet. The vertical segments (fabricated in France) sleeve into each other and are bolted from the interior access shaft. Maintenance is done live (the wires hot with current), and access to the isolators is through the interior shaft that leads to a door at the upper level of the arms (an unprecedented configuration). The arms have a flat, non-slip area with a modular guard rail that flips to a vertical position. The nape of the neck has crampon-like steps for access to the top lightning wire.

EDF Pylons, France

The question of how technology is perceived through design increasingly defines nearly every aspect of contemporary life. High-tech aesthetics sell the gadgetry and furnishings of our daily lives, yet seldom is the same standard of aesthetics applied at the largest scale of regional infrastructure. Girded by surprisingly progressive intentions, in 1992 Electricité de France (EDF) invited an international selection of designers and engineers to submit proposals for a new prototype of overhead high-tension transmission line pylons. The team of Kathryn Gustafson, Ian Ritchie and Henry Bardsley entered into the design process by posing a series of questions to themselves, including (in reference to existing infrastructure), "What does aesthetic poverty communicate to the general public?"

The incremental, invisible lowering of expectations and ensuing inability to perceive true aesthetics – a numbing, in the team's words – that poorly designed public space (including utility infrastructure) wreaks

Each pylon speaks individually rather than as a set of replications. As evidenced by early conceptual sketches (below), the loose gesture of attenuated form responds on a limited basis to its specific surrounds. This is a twist on the typical mass production of infrastructural hardware, in which universal functionality yields formal consistency.

upon the population became the antagonist in the conceptual development of Gustafson, Ritchie and Bardsley's scheme. The design problem of the EDF pylons prototype emerged not simply as an issue of efficiency and formal logic but more profoundly as what the team labeled the "psychology of perception" of progress. Efforts to represent the notion of intertwined technological and cultural progress within the technical parameters of high-tension transmission focused upon shaping a family of objects to interact with a variety of locations and terrain conditions – analogous perhaps to the utility company's efforts to reposition itself as engaged in social and environmental progress beyond its traditional role in an industry driven by economics.

As Sylvain de Bleeckere points out in the project's design documentation, "Real progress for mankind and real future for the earth are becoming the same." Given this, what forms speak of universal optimism

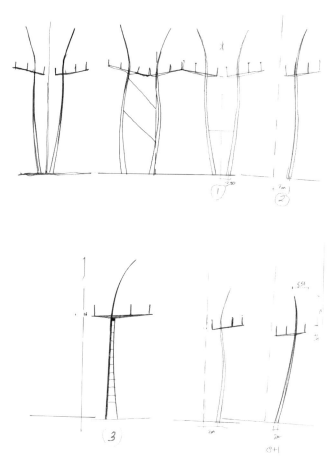

EDF design requirements stated that given the technical constraints of high-tension transmission, there was little room for structural maneuvering. Yet Gustafson, Ritchie and Bardsley of RFR recognize that economy and efficiency do not exclude intelligent redefinition of the role utility structures play in the public landscape. In addition to developing the prototype's form, the design team considered strategic tactics for utility routing and associations of infrastructures. The project raises the question of public astuteness: is the perception of progress possible to attain by repackaging long-existing technologies? Some may see design at the service of sublimation (reworked corporate symbolism), others true aesthetic achievement.

for the future, grounded in awareness of the past and present? Gustafson, Ritchie and Bardsley looked to the imagery of a heron taking flight. Attenuated core verticals hold non-symmetrical, balanced cross pieces that create an armature for high-tension wires. The top of each pylon is pulled into a partial, reaching arc, a visual insinuation of momentary poise yearning for release.

Les Pennes: City Entrance to Marseille

To dream of healing a broken landscape is to practice the weaving of memory and vision. For Kathryn Gustafson, the Pennes-Mirabeau interchange northwest of Marseille is a project that she had coveted for years, a valley floor and hillside ripped open and left mostly unresolved beyond essential engineering solutions. The site is a spaghetti land of on-and off-ramps that splice the heavily trafficked A7 and A55 highways to one another and to local roads. The environmental disruption and potential mending of the landscape have ramifications beyond defining a more memorable link between Marseille and its airport. With the A7 as the primary north-south axis of France and the A55 the major connector between northern Italy and Barcelona, the site operates within the greater transportation infrastructure of the European Union. Given this situation, relating the form, gesture and ecology of the interchange more explicitly to its underlying geography identifies the city and the region within a vast continental network.

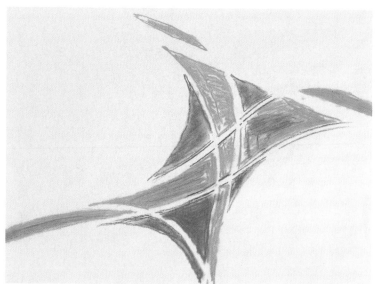

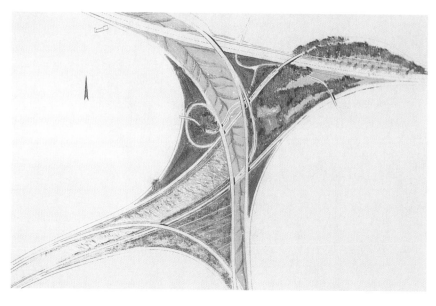

Aerial views (opposite page) display the complex amalgam of highway infrastructure at the entrance to Marseilles. Long before gaining this project commission, Gustafson encountered the interchange first hand on several occasions and was struck by the disrupted landscape. Perspectival renderings (below right) reveal the extent of earth manipulation and contour molding inherent to the original scheme. Secondary to the dramatic land forms, sets of vertical elements (below left, lights and wind turbines, and on pages 48–49, concrete piers) move across the site to clarify directionality and engage in measuring site phenomena such as Mistral winds and storm water collection.

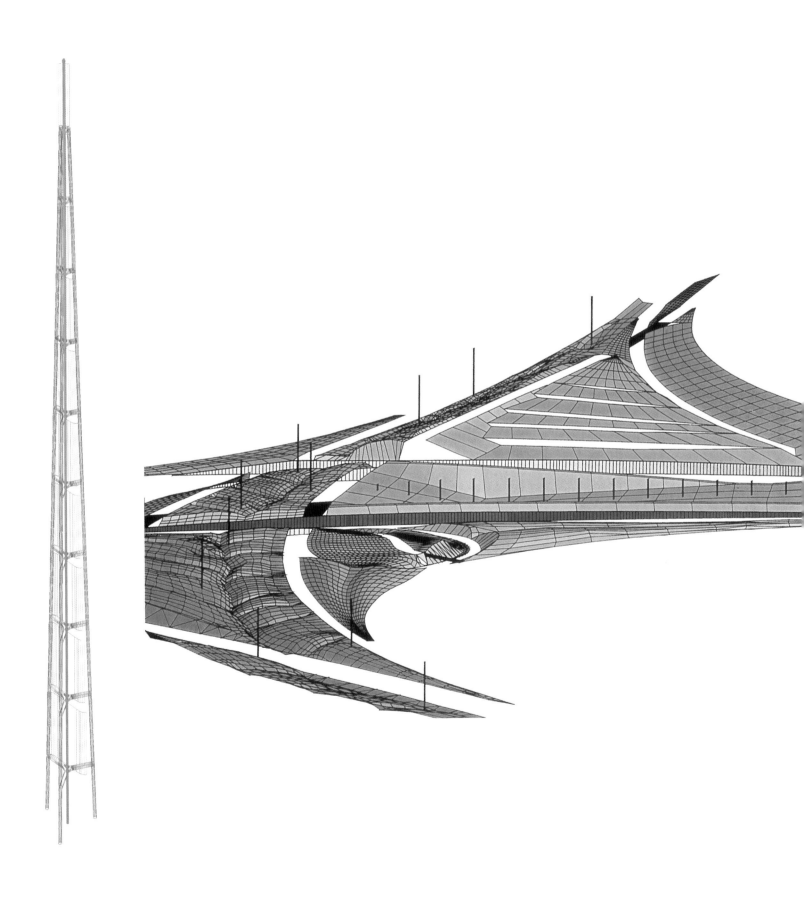

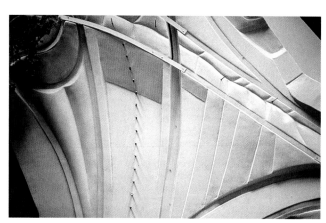

When passing through the gateway, a driver's orientation is first defined and then extended beyond site boundaries by retaining walls (massive gabion metal baskets containing limestone) that strike east-west and the raised figure of the north-south overpass. Shaped to clarify movement patterns but also to conduct storm water run-off from the highways, the scheme's puckered flanks, ravine-like swales, terraced slopes and broad, shallow retention basin offer a variety of microclimates that support diverse plant palettes – some reminiscent of the local Pennes-Mirabeau environment, others of engineered artifice.

From arid mountains that partially ring Marseille, the area drops 100 meters into stretches of *pinède* (pine forest) and olive groves before leveling out in the scenic croplands of the Pennes-Mirabeau valley. This geologic structure becomes a tool of contextualization as two large land movements, one wet and one dry, shape the interchange interstices with 700,000 cubic meters of fill excavated from a nearby tunnel construction. Gustafson initially modeled the design concept with 300 pounds of clay, feeling by hand the land forms that would accept and conduct storm water run-off from the roadways. A matrix of topography (surface topology) and vegetation (surface texture and color) differentiates directional movement through the interchange.

In the dry zone, gabion walls that match the buff-colored stone of the surrounding mountains lift up the land and carry it toward the coastal range. The shallow, elevated valley is incised with angled channels that conduct road run-off into a central spine. As these channels receive moisture, their plant materials grow more vigorously

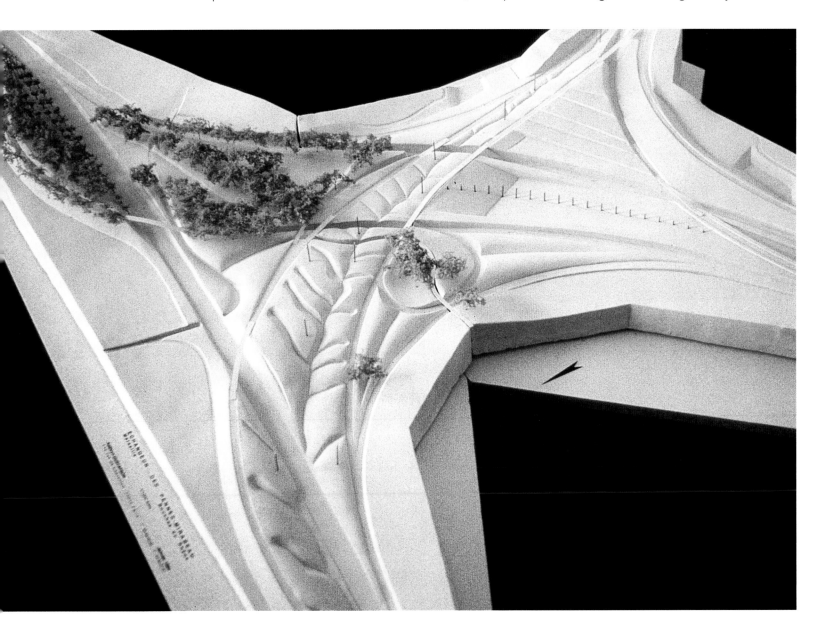

than neighboring shoulders, striking green lines into the blond, bleached grasses of the dry land form. A line of wind turbines were planned to move up the valley into the mountains. Like candles that illuminate with the touch of a flame, the turbines would catch winds and spin fluorescent-edged blades to power small lights.

The wet zone is engineered to accept high volumes of run-off. A line of concrete columns set at varying grades maintain a level plane across their tops as they move up the wet zone, growing in height from 60 centimeters to 18 meters. The concrete sentries make evident the rise and fall of water in the retention basin; they are measuring devices that mark the extent of impervious surface on the surrounding roadways. At the western section of the wet zone, a series of dikes retain water temporarily, allowing run-off to percolate and recharge the water table. Grasses planted between the dikes ripple in the wind like water when the basins are dry. Sections of replanted pine forest and terraced olive groves infill the zone's eastern half. Bracketing the

The growth cycles of plants display contrasting colors, textures and calibrations of movement that bring to life the design scheme. The wet zone is comprised of three distinct environments: flood basin (opposite page), planted with kinetic pampas grass and wildflowers; rough-textured pine forest; and terraced green clouds of olive trees. The dry zone is sheathed in carpets of tall grass (below, in foreground). In season, bright red wedges of poppies splash against the muted tones of the site's grasses, groves and weathered minerals. Far from the traditional notion of garden, the scheme offers arrangements of vegetation that speak at the regional scale.

wet and dry zones, four triangles planted with native wildflowers – featuring poppies that color the fields bright red in season – represent the meadows of southern France. As drivers pass through what would be typically a residual roadside landscape, they are alternately exposed to views of the rich, green growth and water management of the wet zone and the spare, beige beauty of the dry zone. Eight-meter high walls reinforce east-west directionality while north-south movement passes over the walls. Here (and found in other Gustafson projects) earth shaping solves technical issues by engaging water. In turn, water brings life/color/texture that enhances readings of land form. With calm, monumental gestures, the design speaks at the regional scale of the interchange.

Encountering Land

Square Rachmaninov, Quartier de l'Evangile, Paris

Just west of Parc de la Villette in a neighborhood dense with recent medium-rise residential construction, Kathryn Gustafson designed a small park that is of the same generation as La Villette, Parc André Citroën and Parc de Bercy, all works instrumental to the evolution of contemporary landscape architecture. Born from Mitterrand's *grands projets* mandate, these parks hoped to establish new ground for urban open space within the postindustrial paradigm. Like its much larger cohorts, L'Evangile is an overlay of non-perfect but explicit geometries – a squeezed ellipse, a partial bosque, slightly askew cross axes – with site-specific elements: a playground, an arc of pavement and a grand lawn circumscribed by low retaining seating steps that comprise much-needed communal gathering space.

Like much of Gustafson's subsequent work, the park's structure prioritizes reversible social performance spaces, allowing lawn and its raised, paved perimeter to be stage or seating. Also familiar is the use of water

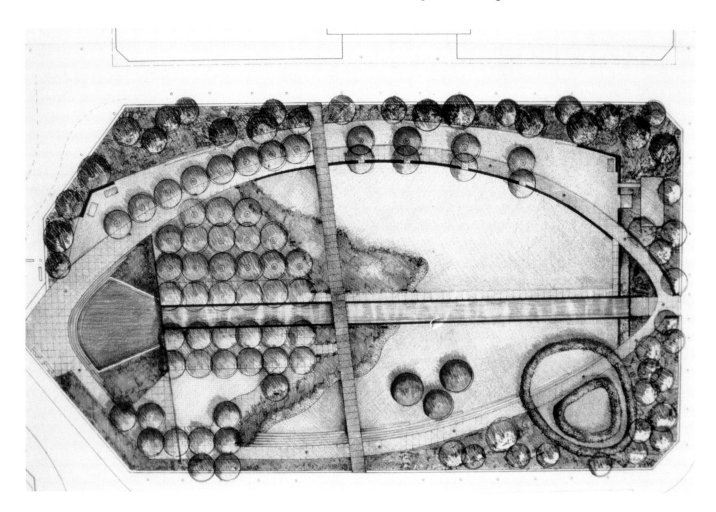

Now known as Square Rachmaninov, given its size, this small city park evokes a surprising variety of spatial and experiential qualities. Set within one city block and tightly surrounded by residential mid-rises the site balances open green space with more defined areas of bosque, grove, promenade and plaza. Small jets express horizontally across the central canal (opposite page, above), activating the water's surface and providing sounds that mask the city context. The scheme's primary element – an oval walk with a stepped inner edge – permits active and passive use to occur simultaneously (image below). The park has limited visual and physical access from adjacent streets but is fully exposed to views from apartments above.

as an organizing element that defines localized spaces within the larger framework. Here the wide canal bisects the length of the park, offering just one crossing and thereby dividing the great lawn and the bosque into paired subspaces that mirror each other but are unequal dimensionally. The canal feeds into a shallow wedge pool that serves as a focal point at the park's primary entrance. The site's boundary is strictly controlled with a fence and gates (typical of Parisian parks) and high, mixed hedges that restrict access to just two major and two minor points.

Plantings are employed as controlled frame but also as a loose infill of seasonal color and texture. A broad stroke of bamboo spills into the smooth lawn at the park's heart. At the site's southeast corner, two nested hedge enclosures set off a privatized zone for play. As one of Gustafson's earliest built works in the public realm, L'Evangile proposes a model for the interaction of urban green space and local residents.

"Landing Pad for Ideas", Paris

In an open competition to celebrate the 200th anniversary of the French Revolution, "Landing Pad for Ideas" was one of 20 out of 700 entries selected for development and display. Kathryn Gustafson located her work along the banks of the Seine in the heart of the 12th arrondissement, grounding the scheme in a linear site that allowed access by foot, bike and barge. "The Revolution was all about ideas to change society," Gustafson explains, and in response, she created a riverside platform for dialog, a landing pad for the cross-fertilization of opinion. The designer also thought about the endurance of women as she designed Landing Pad for Ideas. She was compelled by the sense that through history, women have continued to move forward through emotional and physical challenges. The supportive nature of women was represented in materials such as the strong stone quai edge (consistence) and the soft terraced grass (tenderness).

Elements of the scheme refer to qualities of endurance and receptivity that Gustafson identifies with the female character. A double line of columns marches in procession parallel to the primary walk, each a light beacon that marks a sense of continuity (opposite page). The columns decrease in height until they are flush with the pavement. As the Seine rises, the lights sometimes shine from beneath the water. The columns glow with strength at various heights whether in solitude, inundated with water, or crowded with people. Women are in many ways receivers, and the low mound is a ground swell that accepts force and buffers areas around it from impact (below, plaster model at left).

The scheme features a plot of land at quai level that pushes into the Seine. Set lower than the city streets, the site is on display. Its layout is highly legible both as a spatial sequence (from within) and in plan view (from streets above). A 400-meter promenade lined by light columns traces a center line. From a small grove at the far end of the site, earth wells up and at its height, the land form receives the promenade's push and gathers this into a force of its own. At this moment of thrust and reception, the amphitheater forms a sculptural sweep that opens to the river. Here, where the exchange of site gestures takes place, visitors engage in their own interaction and exchanges. Performances can occur in the amphitheater, over the length of the quai, or on a barge with the audience seated on the molded, linear grass terraces.

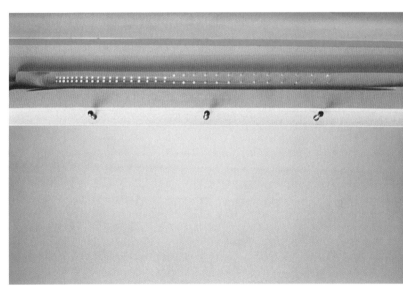

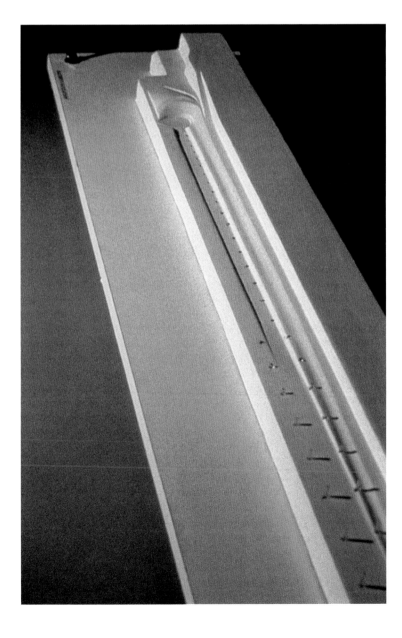

Set against the dramatic roofline and glass façade of the main factory building, a grove of Russian olive trees brings a sense of loose order to the entry sequence that links site to architecture

(below). Although at a distance from the entry walk, the trees' unpredictable postures create visual energy as a sculptural field that is viewed but not entered. Because of the open face of

the research facility buildings and the strength of the inner garden's figural presence, pedestrian circulation reads as a continuous system from outside to inside, one that coexists but never coincides

with the molded terrain (opposite page, lower right). Visitors are brought through billowed berms and across water elements, not merely alongside.

L'Oréal Garden, Aulnay-sous-Bois

At the Barbière factory campus of L'Oréal, tucked into the suburbs between Paris and the Charles-de-Gaulle airport, one finds an early and compact version of Kathryn Gustafson's land sculpting. Inspired by the architects' pre-construction depictions of swooping rooflines and glass curtain walls, Gustafson shaped the inner garden as a thickened horizontal figure that undulates with successive opening movements, as a blossom unfurling. A crucial characteristic of the land form is the idea of refinement: as one moves inward from the entrance, and each time water is crossed, textures and forms gain precision. On the human body, the skin on the outside of the arm is rougher than the tender areas on the inner arm. Most tender of all, the belly of the L'Oréal garden is held within a crooked arm of earth that speaks of force and fragility.

The first elements of the entry sequence are two groves, one a thick line of ginkgos that screen a busy avenue and the other an orchard of Russian Olive trees planted in front of the magnificent wave of

The plaster model (below, right) showcases a dialog between land and built form. Tellingly (and typical of Gustafson's practice), the monochromatic models are unadorned: materiality is secondary to interaction of form and figural gesture. Once defined, however, materials play an important role in the scheme's *parti* as plantings transition from rough to fine textures, moving inward, and concrete gives way to more refined copper to retain earth (below, left and upper right). The tectonics of the garden's frame – the transparency of the curtain walls – is crucial to site experience. The central pool speaks about cleansing and purification, actions inherent to L'Oréal's cosmetics research; it is also a reservoir for the campus sprinkler system.

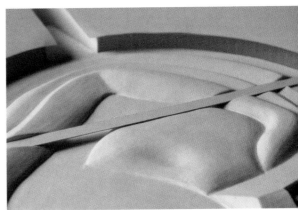

Valode & Pistre's glass façade. As the entry walk moves from parking toward the reception wing, one passes through a series of linear mounds that alternate with carpets of red rose bushes. The angular mounds, like outer rings most distant from the point that a pebble drops into a pond, foreshadow the inner rings although lack the core's focused energy. Moving inward, coarse shrubs segue to ground covers and finally to turf. Land form becomes more highly resolved, and the research facility's pursuit of precision, science and beauty comes to mind.

At the heart of the garden, an off-center pool separates bodies of land and slips beneath one edge of the reception wing at its broadest point. Fed by steep sided runnels, the low, still pool gives the sense that surrounding land form emerged over time from primordial waters. This in turn enhances an unexpected ambiguity of scale: the emergent, swelled and molded topographies – subtle, rhythmic and non-regular –

Crisp detailing enhances reading of sculpted land form. As one moves along the boardwalk and through the interiors adjacent to the garden, the undulating ground plane prevents a singular reading of site relationships. Visitors must re-orient themselves based on a flow of changing perceptions of scale and organization. Nine magnolias and small seating areas punctuate the inner garden turf, providing moments of pause more integrated into the landforms than the hovering boardwalk. In the original design, a botanical garden sat between the reception wing and factory building, anchoring one end of the primary board-walk. Color bands parallel to the path of the sun were planted with varieties used by L'Oréal's research teams.

make reference to micro and macro (or local and global) movements simultaneously. Cutting across the width of the inner garden, a hardwood boardwalk carries foot traffic in a direct line that contrasts with the surrounding topography. Rather than using the hardened surface of primary walkways to frame the movement of contours and water, as happens at the nearby corporate gardens of Esso and Shell, here the circulation directly intersects undulating topography, not disrupting but asserting itself as a coexisting system. There is a sense of removal that implies distance and great dimension within a relatively small space. The land forms, set below eye level, modulate but do not obscure views across the garden. One is drawn down into the landscape as a small figure within the thickened surface.

Shell Headquarters Garden, Rueil-Malmaison

From the *ferme ornée* (ornamental farm) rooted in the tradition of Roman agricultural estates to opulent royal gardens, from grand civic boulevards to civil engineering projects that put entire natural systems at the disposal of a nation's appetite for energy, humans have used land as a resource of power, productivity and pleasure. With the rise of corporate campuses in the post-war period, designed landscapes in addition to signature architecture became a means to establish and reinforce commercial identities. While many corporate landscapes look to the model of classic gardens to communicate organizational strength and prestige, some seek more contemporary expressions. In the late 1980s, Shell Petroleum hired Kathryn Gustafson to create a distinctive entry court and campus landscape for a new headquarters complex designed by architectural firm Valode & Pistre.

The international headquarters campus uses bold landscape to present a distinctive corporation identity. But the everyday spaces that employees inhabit and visitors encounter matter too. The entry is a monumental and memorable court of spare stone and water that lies at the foot of ascending, rippling ground form (opposite page, and upper left of site plan below, top half). Between the building wings pocket gardens provide intimate areas for lunchtime enjoyment and seasonal compositions viewed from the offices above (in the site plan below, bottom half). An aquatic garden is found at the heart of the site.

In preliminary discussions with the client and architects, Gustafson identified three primary campus landscapes and their associated campus programming: international (the entry court); community (the aquatic garden); and private (the pocket gardens). The entry court is about the earth and industry's relationship to oil: the grass represents fluid oil, the walls are the rocks of fossilized minerals, water and the columns refer to the refinement process. The Aquatic Garden, in this interpretation, is a thought about the better life that we lead due to the comforts that extractive energies offer us. Between the wide stone entry walk and the east wing of the building complex, a shallow pool runs the length of the space. The pool is still and reflective, its surface broken down the middle by a low pour-over that aerates the water. Four stainless steel masts rise out of the pool, succinctly punctuating the horizontal plane. The water level is perceived to be nearly even with the entry walk and with the building's main floor, giving the impression that stone and water integrate

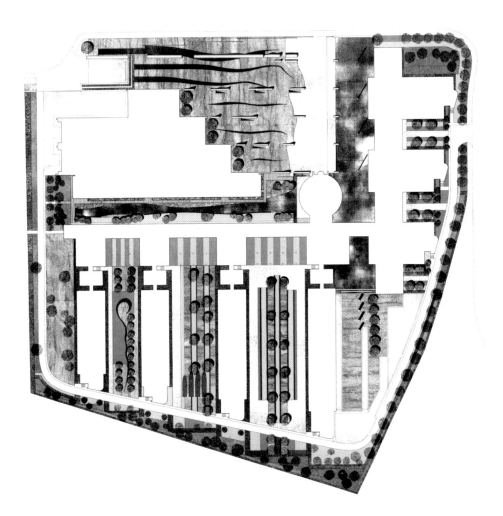

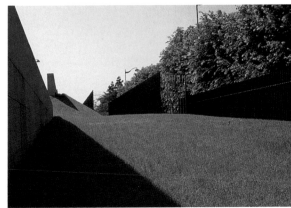

architecture and environment as a constant base plane throughout the site. This impression is strengthened when the pool slips out of sight beneath structure at its southern end.

Along the west side of the entry court, fat ribbons of lawn well upward from the walkway. An early and outstanding example of Gustafson's mastery of manipulation of perceptual space using sculpted land, the undulating contours are interpretive – they link the entry court to Shell's business of industrial oil exploration with their fluid quality – and utilitarian, as they disguise parking and mechanical structures below grade.

The lawn panels move high above eye level, and are far from the obedient parterres one might expect to encounter at an office park. With this presentation of outsized, unexpected scale, the relationship of (a visitor's) body to the experience of place is forcibly enhanced. The Aquatic Garden is located just west and one story below the freestanding lobby, set deep between two bars of the corporate complex. A shaded,

The pale stone entry court is framed by a 1,860 square meters rectangle of water along its east side and sculpted waves of lawn punctured by low limestone walls to the west (opposite page, looking west). Close coordination with project architects was needed to incorporate parking structure access stairs, ventilation shafts and utility vaults into the contours of the steeply undulating lawn (below, left). The entry pool is bisected by a seven-centimeter drop that visually activates the surface while aerating the shallow water (below, right). The finished floor elevation of adjacent interior spaces hovers just above water level, creating interaction with the reflective glass façade.

linear space, the garden has a subliminal quality to it, a sort of primordial explosion in the ordered suburban campus. The garden is visible from the lobby and building entry hall, the cafeteria, overhead offices and a pedestrian bridge. Seasonal blooms activate the lush, green reeds and shrub plantings. If any aspect of the overall scheme plays to optical entertainment or romantic garden traditions, it is here, at the heart of the corporate community.

Described by Gustafson as the private zone of the master plan, on the back or south side of the complex three pocket gardens stretch the length of four office wings. Although sharing common components of bands of grass, ground covers and shrubs, each garden has an individual character or theme. All three bloom in one color, either white, yellow and red, similar colors as found in the nearby Aquatic Garden. There are also two additional pocket gardens, based on blue foliage and blossoms, on the east side. Conceived to

Tucked as a lush gorge between the two major campus blocks, the Aquatic Garden is fed by a cascade issued from the entry pool (opposite page). The garden is directly accessible via a boardwalk, but its primary purpose is as a scenic element. It is a romantic interlude of flowering shrubs and water lilies distinct from the contemporary minimalist character of the encompassing campus, seemingly clipped from a wetland and stitched into the corporate landscape. The back pocket gardens are ordered into bands of grass, ground covers and shrubs that extend the architectural grid (below). Each features a color that also appears in the adjacent Aquatic Garden (the two areas are separated but equally visible from an elevated internal corridor).

provide intimate spaces for lunchtime breaks and to enliven views from within office cubicles, the pocket gardens are seen and used by a limited population.

Shell Petroleum is one of Gustafson's first big corporate commissions. In discussing the project and its design process, the designer recalls the enthusiasm with which the client entered into the landscape development, proposing at one point to purchase a nursery's entire stock. In turn, she says that she learned much about being methodical, about effectively crossing back and forth over the line between intuitive design expression and the rational communication standards essential to any project's success. The results are evident in the finished product: a campus landscape that melds conceptual framing and bold design with the complexities of a corporation's dual public/private functionality.

Esso Headquarters Garden, Rueil-Malmaison

Moving in measured paces from building to river, the Esso Headquarters corporate garden answers to multiple contexts. There is the immediate architectural context of Viguier and Jodry's modernist-inspired headquarters. There is the site context, which brings both natural and cultural ingredients into play along the banks of the Seine River on the outskirts of Paris, where centuries of painters recorded the progress of industry and art. And finally, there are nested conceptual contexts, from the local (how does a private, corporate landscape meet a public river way and popular pedestrian path system?) to the global (how does one approach the design of a garden for a multi-national petrochemical giant?).

   Kathryn Gustafson describes the design of the Esso garden as an investigation into a new kind of urbanity, one that mediates between dominant architectural objects and the much larger scale of the natural environment. The scheme is an exercise in reducing an array of complex relationships to a set of simplified

Viewed from the upper floors of the Esso Headquarters building (opposite page), two layers of the garden are apparent: serial narrow canals that define the ground plane in relation to Viguier and Jodry's architectural frame, and a sprinkling of tree canopies that blend the site into the banks of the Seine. From this vantage point, the willow's silvery-green foliage softens the garden's ordered framework and provides a contextualizing color palette. As seen from the riverside path (below), the cascade is a horizontal gesture that reflects the building's circulation core onto the site. The directional flow of the shallow cascade reaches toward the Seine, implying a connection that segues from architecturalized to naturalized water, from new to old.

gestures. Also, in the designer's words, it is "about what you reveal, what you hide, what comes to light." While the minimalist instinct is common to many of Gustafson and partners' projects, the explicit legibility of ordered versus organic found at Esso is not.

The garden's primary structural lines are drawn by a series of narrow, marble-edged canals that run perpendicularly into a shallow cascade. The cascade extends along one wing of the building's L-shaped mass, visually uniting architecture and garden. The positioning, dimensions and reflectivity of the cascade mirror the glass curtain wall of the headquarter's circulation core, allowing interior gathering spaces to be echoed on the exterior as water cleanly links the ground floor lobby to a paved plaza at the river's edge.

Within this framework, subtle billows of land undulate diagonally across the site. The land movement marks shadows cast by the building on the solstice and the equinox, incorporating reference to cycles far

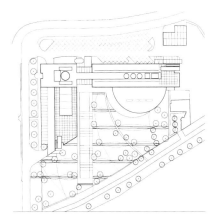

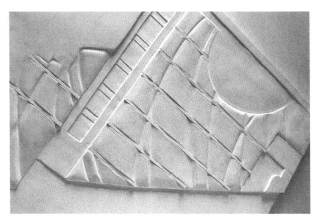

The cascade apron (below) is stepped along one side and ramped along the other. This reinforces the perception of the pavement sitting nearly flush with the water's surface. The effect gives visitors an intimate experience of the slow-moving water and of textural stone as the shallow depth enriches the mineral colors. The cascade is fed by the canals that slice across the site's contours (opposite page, bottom) and feed their tributary waters into the main pool via inlets set beneath the stepped apron. The site plan and original schematic plaster model (opposite page, top) reveal the interweaving of organic topography and orthogonal water features.

beyond corporate, suburban, and urban conditions. Swells of turf catch the eye as they respond to but are not halted by the orthogonal order of the canals. Tucked against the south wing, an employee café opens onto a semisphere plaza that pushes into the garden. Around the garden's perimeter, boundaries are clearly marked by a stone retaining wall and clipped hedge.

It's possible to walk out between pastoral groupings of willow trees, to traverse the low, rounded land forms and follow the narrow channels that are alternately embedded into and elevated above the shifting ground plane. But the garden doesn't call for physical engagement to be fully experienced or understood. Most of the story is told by the eye, although the outcome of the story differs according to the viewer's orientation. Viewed from above, the sensual coherency of the land movement against the ordered garden structure is more apparent than from inside the space. Seen from across the river (at the scale of the river),

Directly adjacent to the headquarters is a small public garden alongside the pedestrian path (opposite page). Double curve formed steel Earth Slicers retain the lawn grade to create a planting area. The gesture of the steel arc extends the overall site plan and connects to a waterside resting area (below). On a deck cantilevered over the Seine sit two sculptural benches. Also of formed steel varnished after developing a layer of rust, the Water Gazers have a hand-pounded surface and hold two people. These public spaces are small insertions that are strikingly contemporary within the pastoralism of this section of the Seine, a symptom of suburban corporate developments that jostle fenced-in grounds against the banks of the historic waterway.

the presence of willows naturalizes and historicizes the garden's contemporary precision as silvery foliage melds into the plant palette along the banks of the Seine. Within the garden, from the suburban comfort of the canal's stone apron or at the sweep of the café terrace, the eye is drawn to the motion of slow flowing water, to the familiar textures of grass and foliage, and to the kinetic, irregular *bas relief* of the lawn's modulations.

Severely polluted and destined to be capped, the site was approached by Gustafson as a manipulation of horizontal surface into a figural composition (below early conceptual diagrams and schematic model). The designer's scheme for "Housing in the Park," the competition program, is not directly replicated in other works but its solution is: carved land form controls perception and use of space. Here, residential zones (4.2 hectares) are separated from park land (8.8 hectares) by retaining the floor level 1.5 meter above the public ground and by enclosing parking under a pergola. Security concerns are met without interrupting the fluid composition of land movement, allowing the site to read as an integrated whole.

Thames Barrier Park, London

The co-creation of private housing and public open space presents a challenge that persists through time in the making and re-making of cities. In 1995, Kathryn Gustafson explored this issue in the Thames Barrier Park competition. In the designer's mind, the Dockland's location offered an "irreplaceable sensual dimension" brought about by history interacting with tidal fluctuations, wind, sun and rain on the river's surface. Implicit in the solution was the use of sculptural land movement and lighting to differentiate zones. Although unbuilt, the scheme had several critical strands rooted in earlier projects that impacted subsequent work. The first was scale. Gustafson created a large arrival promontory walk that met the size of the river and announced views to the Thames Barrier. The sensory impact of weather and climate, a second thematic strand, influenced elements such as the inlet's sectional profile, the pontoon and the performance area.

Without pretense of idealized nature or romanticized city, aspects of the docklands and the movement of boats inspired design features that allow direct experience of big water in the urban setting.

Features attractive to both residential inhabitants and visitors are located in prime areas, including an exhibition/restaurant building and a performance space oriented to take advantage of river

views and to protect from cold northeast winds. Although relatively grand in perceptual scale (due to land gesture and the strong presence of urban/natural infrastructures), the park

offers intimate and dynamic interaction between land and water: a sense of stretching outward without interruption as the site transitions from private to public, from city to river, from past to present.

Swiss Cottage Open Space, London

The spirit or soul of a place – its *genus loci* – is derived from physical attributes, site history, and the habits of its users. In a public space, connection to a specific context has to do with facilitating interaction between groups and individuals whose needs and interests change over time. At Swiss Cottage on Avenue Road in Camden, Gustafson Porter designed a small park surrounded by buildings of local importance – a community center, a theater, a sports center, offices, affordable housing, luxury housing and a home for the elderly – into an open space that eloquently mixes the evolving cultural and recreational needs of a diverse neighborhood with subtle grace. The Swiss Cottage Open Space is one of four landscape projects which are interlinked, including: the Swiss Cottage Library entrance, the Eton Avenue market, and the Leisure Centre landscape. In coordination with these related projects and new architectural elements, the scheme updates a collection of loosely related functions into a coherent, communal setting with an elevated sense of place.

The local community has changed significantly since the original park was built in the 1970s and Gustafson Porter hope to make a space inclusive of the increasingly diverse community that is informal, active and theatrical. Unusual for a public park in England, the plant palette features a large amount of clipped structural hedges. The herbaceous perennials are collections of British native varieties mixed with hybrids and exotics embedded in British culture (such as the English rose). The plantings are based on collective memory, types that people know from childhood to encourage acceptance of the space as a new home. Camden as a borough is committed to noteworthy planting in their parks and has been supportive of the design's intentions.

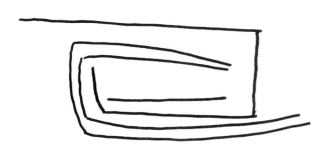

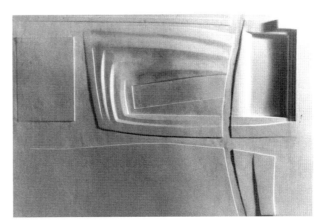

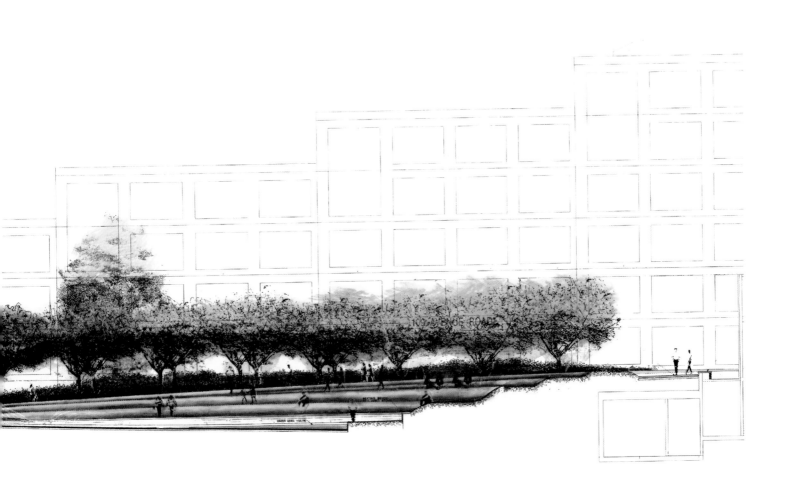

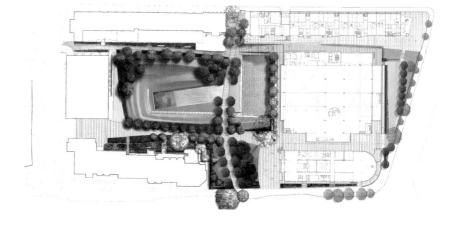

At the park's heart is an interactive water feature intended for play as well as visual drama. Thin streams of water emit from jets set at thirty-degree angles and course down a rectangular, sloping plane embedded into softly stepped grass banks. The textured, granite surface captures water and conducts it as a rippling sheet into a shallow pool. The flow can be turned off to allow the paved surface to host large gatherings. Like other projects of Gustafson and partners, the presence and absence of water accommodates (and signals) activity and tranquility with equal ease. Molded land form and lush plantings frame the water element, evoking the luxuries of a garden that stands out from the typical, publicly funded neighborhood park. The land form responds to sun angles and to the eye's love of graceful undulations as much as to issues of access and utility. Stretches of open turf are used as an amphitheater for public events; smaller areas defined by plantings around the perimeter provide more private moments. Throughout the site, the juxtaposition of ground levels

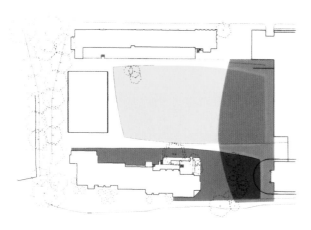

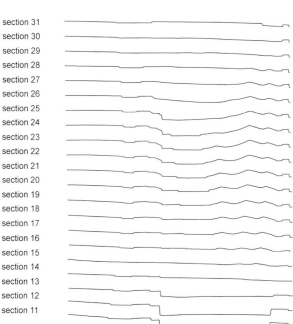

section 31
section 30
section 29
section 28
section 27
section 26
section 25
section 24
section 23
section 22
section 21
section 20
section 19
section 18
section 17
section 16
section 15
section 14
section 13
section 12
section 11

In concert with the rich plant palette, the central water feature and sensual land modeling define the Swiss Cottage Open Space. Large activity areas such as the amphitheater (adjacent to a new theater and school of drama) balance with intimate pockets set into green alcoves. The central water feature, pushes softly into land form in a manner that engages the eye down into the site and encourages discovery (perspective sketch below). The primary north-south pathway of creamy yellow granite and east-west path of medium gray granite organize the park into coherent sub-spaces. Diagrams illustrate the scheme's interlocking areas (page 74), and preliminary sections taken from digital scans of the clay model (page 76, bottom).

offers opportunities for performance (athletic or aesthetic) and observation at varying scales. Two cross-axial pedestrian paths link the major venues that enclose the open space, dividing the site into unequal portions.

Lines and groves of trees reinforce the scheme's organization, framing circulation and major open areas. A sunken sports pitch occupies the southern sector of open space with a level surface that contrasts with the movement of the adjacent sculpted earth and ephemeral water. Like water, a simple lighting strategy serves both as an agent whose presence and absence define spatial parameters and as a phenomenological tool that contributes to atmospheric effects. With clipped precision, plantings go beyond the expected display of seasonal interest and play an important role in outlining spatial volume in concert with land form and water. With hopes to create an open space that is functional, progressive and poetic, the design looks to the future of Swiss Cottage.

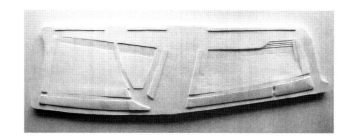

North End Parks, Boston

The transformation of types from one scale to another can cause twists in the interpretation of form, use and meaning. In Gustafson Guthrie Nichol's scheme for the North End Parks in Boston, two elements – threshold and porch – are enlarged to fit the city's dimensions such that they are experienced as urban spatial infrastructure. The inverse is also true: the elements are a reductive lens that knits sectors of Boston's modern downtown to its historic North End neighborhood of low-rise dwellings and narrow, stone streets. The guiding concept behind GGN's scheme, "from city to home," responds to intertwined political and physiographical strands of site history. The parks occupy two halves of an arced rectangle reclaimed by Boston's decade-long Big Dig project. The grounds are one segment of the Rose Kennedy Greenway, a new linear open space system that now lies atop buried lanes of Interstate 93.

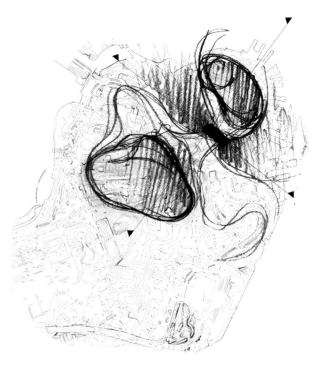

Above the water scrim a porch for North Enders connects southward to other Greenway parks at three scales: City, Neighborhood and Park. Plant palettes segue from species intended to invoke nostalgia for ancestral lands to newer varieties that represent the vitality of today's North End inhabitants. Tree canopies emphasize the threshold between neighborhood and city skyline. The ground plane dips and rises to reinforce a sense of entry and acceptance into the site. A single walkway angles across the north park following the original Salem Street axis.

Like the entire greenway, the existence of the North End Parks is a testament to a moment at which the city completed massive reconstructive surgery. But the design *parti* speaks also to an earlier phase of topological morphing when the old North End was an isolated point connected to the city by a thin neck of land. Over the course of years, nearby hills were shaved down to fill tidal lands and widen the neck into many blocks of tenable terrain. The parks' combined form is a threshold recalling a time when Hanover Street served as the only crossing ground between downtown and the immigrant settlement of the North End. A tilted water scrim spans the parks, making reference to the Middlesex canal that once served the North End from Boston proper. Transition from city to home is enabled both by the historic geophysical process and by a contemporary realignment of urban infrastructure.

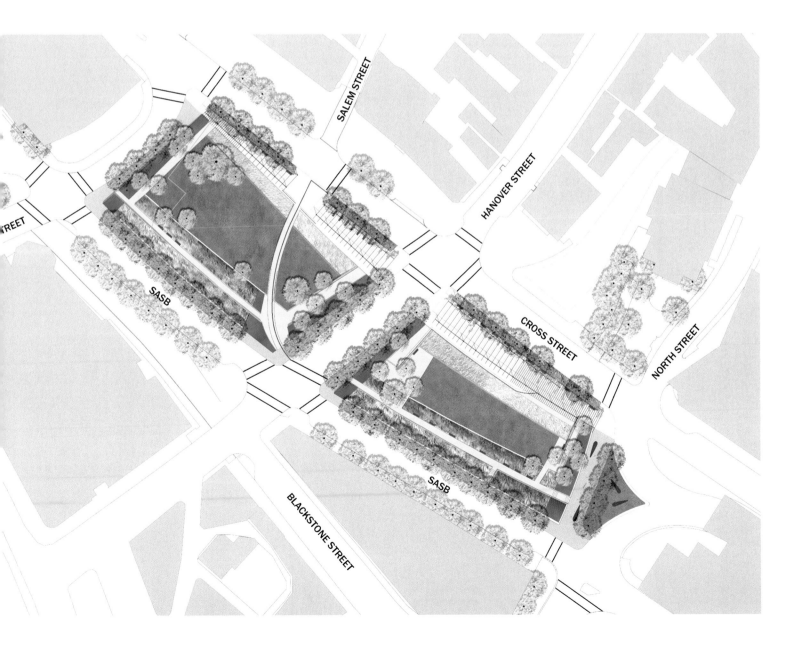

Light and Water

Equally a reference line, a retaining wall and a balcony, the Dragon Pool moves in angular segments across the site's upper level (opposite page and below). The pool creates individual sub-plazas for the city hall, the cathedral and other public buildings and anchors the civic complex by holding the grade up above the main square below. The water body is cut through diagonally by a stair on axis between the city hall and the train station across the street. A silent, reflective element from above, from within the plaza, the green granite walls of the basin – 15 centimeters thick and each about five by two meters – assert a formal presence that defines one side of the open space.

Rights of Man Square, Evry

Complex sites call for complex solutions, although in Kathryn Gustafson's view, complexity is not necessarily the opposite of simplicity. When Gustafson won the competition for the Rights of Man Square in 1989, the existing site conditions included a train station, a heavily trafficked national highway along the north boundary and an awkward south-to-north fall line with a collection of civic buildings at the height of land (including the city hall and Mario Botta's cathedral). Like master brush strokes that render a busy scene with a gesture or two, efficient reordering of the site section transformed competing connection and orientation issues into a spatially unified structure.

Gustafson's first move was to break the plaza's existing slope into four topographical elements: a plinth, an inclined plane, a leveled area and a set of site-scaled seat steps. With integrated retaining walls and subtle grade changes, the scheme deals with the complexities of underground parking access and a mixed context

The Movement Pool runs perpendicularly into the White Wall at its east end (below left), creating a platform for the Signal Wall, one of two pedestrian access points into the parking below grade. A slot cut into the White Wall at eye level frames views down over the Movement Pool (below left and opposite page above). The slot lets western sun and the sound of cascading water into the parking structure, blending boundaries between above and below ground and allowing users to map sensory clues about where they park. Atop the White Wall, the custom designed "Siège" (seat/guard rail) is a sculptural piece that invites passersby to pause, lean elbows on the formed metal cap and observe the plaza.

while setting up dynamic conditions for sight lines, movement, and public interaction. Conceptually grounded in the notion of "freedom of expression" (from the French constitution's Rights of Man), through its sectional relationships the design scheme facilitates civic interaction and cultural performance.

The upper plinth anchors and connects assorted public buildings and the cathedral. It also provides a balcony for passers-by and daily users to pause and observe the plaza below. The plaza is fully open to the public, but the plinth allows separation between types of users if needed. From the base of the plinth, an inclined plane descends at three percent toward the site's center. This element acts as both a stage and a viewing platform without sacrificing its utilitarian function of connecting one site elevation to the next. At the toe of the incline, the plaza levels out momentarily before rising from the north side in a broad set of seat steps. Similarly to the inclined plane, the seat steps have a flexible purpose: they are intended both to be

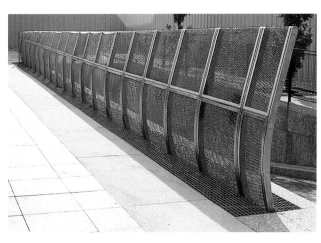

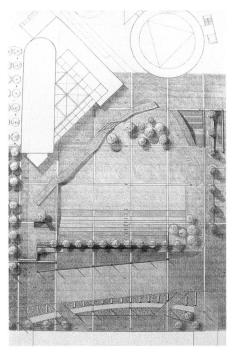

looked at and looked out from. Generous steps in public spaces often by default become places for people to perch. Here, the designer plays up this tendency by stretching the steps the width of the plaza.

A defining aspect of this urban space is its sheer scale created with minimal ingredients (primarily stone, water, and light). Over one hectare/two and a half acres of granite-paved surface immediately raises the question of how to avoid the impression of emptiness. Occurring relatively early in Gustafson's practice, the resolution of this question led to the development of a design strategy whose lineage can be traced to a number of subsequent projects. Specifically, water is used as site phenomenon that allows a single space to have alternate identities or moods, to cycle through periods of intense activity and light usage while never being truly full nor empty. At Evry, the Plage des Jets (beach of jets), a field of 153 recessed nozzles located at the heart of the plaza, reads physically as sculptural form and perceptually as ambient atmosphere. The jets

At the southwest corner of the plaza (site plan, page 85), the Grand Stair carries people up from the parking level directly on axis with Mario Botta's cathedral alongside a line of columnar oaks.

Crossing over the Grand Stair, a pedestrian bridge (page 85, top right) with custom moiré infill (stainless steel mesh layered in various gauges to gather and reflect light) directs perspectival sight lines toward the cathedral. Site furniture and lighting are custom-designed by Gustafson's office. The *Plage des Jets* (below and opposite page) allows the square to be "full when empty, empty when full." Catching sunlight by day and illuminated at night, the jets vocalize daily site cycles and can be turned off for activities.

are programmed to emit thin, waving streams, "fences and grasses" that key into the site's agricultural history. It is a presence that can disappear and reappear, an ephemeral environment of sound, light and motion that responds to its use. Elsewhere on site water is used as a stationary element to define specific relationships, such as the Dragon Pool that runs along the edge of the upper plinth and the Movement Pool that sits at the site's low point, marking the central open space. More than a featured effect, the presence or absence of water literally alters the site's spatial parameters.

The custom-designed wind chime sculptures rise out of the Silver Field section of the garden. Although in an urban setting, the pieces read against the drama of lake and mountains, heightening their delicate angular form. Visually reminiscent of street lighting, the sculptures are not out of place in the city, yet their very function (as wind chimes) alerts visitors to the forces of nature such as wind movement and sun. An assortment of silver-foliaged plants articulates the ground plane beneath the sculptures, activating a horizontal field out of which rise the vertical elements.

Wind and Sound Garden, Lausanne

In the 1990s, garden festivals of a new sort gained in popularity. Moving beyond traditional floral displays geared to the horticultural industry and into territory more closely aligned with installation and performance works from the art world, the new festivals frequently were themed around topics intended to push the boundaries of landscape architecture. Various festivals continue to extend and, some say, distort the culture, materiality, functionality and definition of gardens, trading permanence and programmatic justification for short-term provocation. In 1997, at the first annual Festival du Jardin Urbain in Lausanne, Kathryn Gustafson collaborated with composer François Paris on an installation. The two hoped to map wind patterns with sound sculptures and shimmering plants.

Along the Esplanade de Montbenon above Lake Léman, a broad terrace offers views of glittering water backed by the steep rise of the Alps. In an initial site visit, Gustafson noted that although spectacular, the

space lacked a sense of framing that might anchor experience to place. When working with spatial volume there is a fine line between the instinct to intensify and the will to control to the point of deadening. Perhaps aware of this, the designer sought the insight of composer Paris with questions of how to frame space with sonar qualities instead of fixed elements. With intentions to make visitors aware of both nature and the city when on site, the scheme brings character to the terrace with sound devices (sculptures) and plantings of dramatic texture and color.

In addition to the atmospheric qualities of sound and texture, four types of objects placed with a minimalist's sensibility contribute to restructuring perception of the site: wind chimes, echo chambers, an allée of glass bells, and a water gong. Guided through the lakeside promenade by the visual curiosity of these elements, visitors are simultaneously exposed to sounds the devices produce when played by the

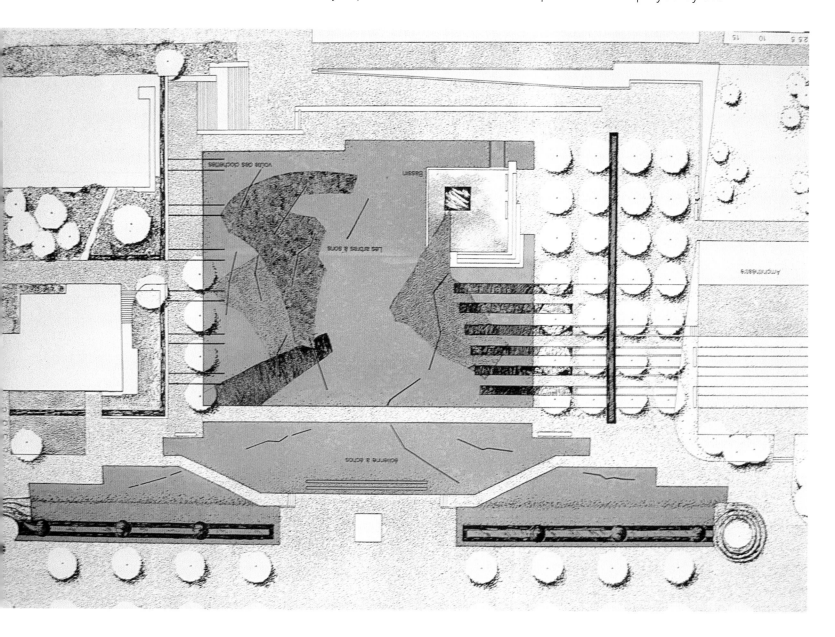

The garden is comprised of three major areas (site plan, opposite page). From left to right are the Silver Field, the Water Gong, and the Glass Bell Allée which slices symmetrically through a gridded bosque of trees. The Silver Field color palette is based on the site's natural context, accentuated by new plantings with silver foliage. Together, Gustafson intends, the silver plantings and the sound sculptures "meld into a harmony of sound, light, texture and color, blurring and marring the boundaries of man and nature." The Glass Bell Allée (detail shot below) is framed by and separated from the rest of the garden by linear plant beds saturated with blue plants (page 89, Echo Chamber sculpture in foreground).

winds along the boundary of land and lake. By modifying sonar ambiance and gently framing the panoramic view with swathes of vegetation, the scale of the site's surrounding is harnessed to become a place-specific performance, an act of urban nature.

Seattle Civic Center

Occupying three city blocks and negotiating 80 feet of elevation, the Seattle Civic Center's open space plan defies traditional notions of the civic plaza as centered, hierarchical or even fully exterior. Instead, the scheme integrates public space and municipal architecture in a multi-level arc of civic moments strung together by water, stone and glass. A grand stair, accompanied by a cascade of water, cuts through City Hall and elevates the experience of streetscape and building interior above pedestrian expectations and into the realm of discovery. The water course provides an analog for the city's geography: Seattle is perched on hills that deliver drainage flowing from the Cascade Mountains into Elliot Bay. Throughout the site, quartzite underfoot and limestone walls orient views according to the colors of the bay and the city's predominant architectural material. Illuminated glass in the form of wall-mounted panels (Justice Center façade), a structural bridge (City Hall interior) and translucent curtain walls (Fourth Avenue plaza) call out important points along the civic sequence.

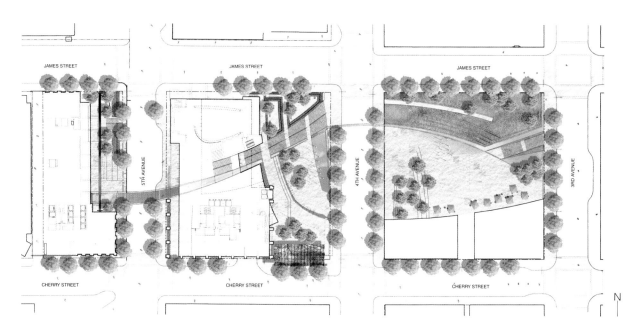

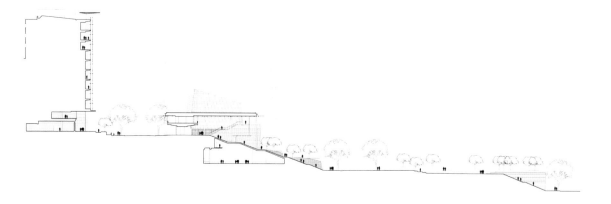

Descending through the site (from left to right in the plan and section on the opposite page), visitors are guided by the scheme's three unifying elements – water, stone and glass. The journey begins at the Justice Center, passes through City Hall, down the Grand Stair, and out to the plaza. Early in conceptual design it became clear that the stair needed to move through City Hall as an indoor/outdoor element to accommodate the steep existing grade. Across Fourth Avenue, the plaza expands with a grass amphitheater along its south side (top right and opposite page). The plaza's gentle warp in plan and section allows a flexible perception of spatial volume.

A major challenge of the project is how to create a vertical promenade that moves people up and down the steep hillside, and between three sectors of civic campus, without resorting to the familiar but limiting escalator and elevator solution. In the existing site section, the City Hall block has a 17-percent slope, east to west, which presents serious access issues. The design team artfully reconstructed the slope into upper and lower platforms (at Fifth Avenue and Fourth Avenue grades, respectively), and connected the platforms with the arc sweep of the grand stair. GGN and Bohlin collaborated to ensure that the gesture reads coherently, and indeed it does, to such an extent that the cascade stair slips out of easy building/site or object/field dialectics. The stair is urbanized topography, an independent urban form that is both sculptural figure and prioritized ground.

Water and illumination issue from the Justice Center's west façade (on the opposite page, these elements occur at the far left). Beginning here, on horizontal surfaces quartzite has the slate blue, greenish gray shimmer of Elliot Bay, reminiscent of gazing from atop Seattle's hills down into the Sound (these pages and page 93). Vertical faces are sheathed with a light limestone, akin to what the eye catches when looking up from the bay at the city spread over hilltops. At the Justice Center, a stepped plant bed holds visitors back from the raised edge of the terrace (below).

Art glass, long a part of Northwestern craft tradition, broadens the contextual underpinnings of the design scheme. At the site's height, a modular yellow glass screen mounted vertically at the entrance to the Justice Center (opposite page) casts a startling glow into the building's circulation core, a hyper burst of solar-like illumination in a region of low light. The light interacts with activated water which bubbles up from between submerged panels. From this headwater pool, water follows the flow of people through the length of the site. Water courses along a channel cut into the lobby floor of City Hall, beneath a blue glass bridge by artist James Carpenter and alongside the Grand Stair.

The project's second major challenge has to do with meeting Seattle's desire for a downtown gathering area that is accessible by public transit, inviting outside of business hours, and not dominated by commercial concerns. Along the east side of Fourth Avenue, the designers opened up a multi-tiered plaza that receives the grand stair. The plaza expands across the avenue (the city's main parade street) into an open space with a grassy amphitheater sized to host major events and connections to public transit below grade. Trees, lighting and a zone of recessed water jets puncture the plaza's surface. Combined with the gentle warping of land form in plan and section, a flexible perception of spatial volume is created. For the future of this civic campus, the presence of moving water, coded stone and illuminated glass are important seeds for the cultivation of safe, interactive public space. The embedding of site circulation as an urban-scaled gestural sweep through City Hall takes advantage of rather than succumbs to challenging infrastructural issues.

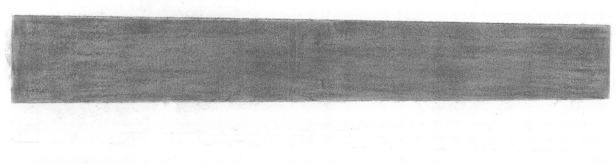

1/100 m2   July 2, oo   M4
CH Red wall ELEVATION

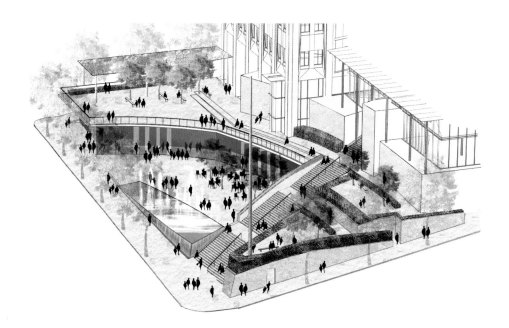

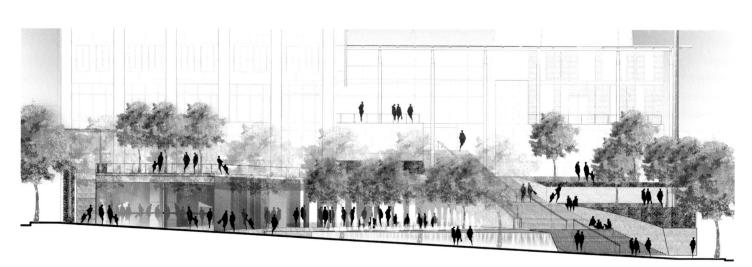

One block west and three stories below the Justice Center, the Sun Wall emits a red hue that recalls classic Seattle sunsets (below and opposite). The single-height curtain of illuminated red glass moves north-south across the City Hall plaza to enclose an interior circulation corridor, retail space and an arts café. This completes the three primary colors of glass in reference to the three primary branches of government. Across Fourth Avenue (see plan, page 92) the flow of water continues from a shallow scrim toward the bay. At the edge of the plaza elevated above Third Avenue, water drops into a cascade stair and descends to passenger platforms in the commuter tunnel below grade, connecting above and below ground with light and water.

An American and Pacific Northwest icon, the Space Needle (opposite page) rises from the heart of the Seattle Center and is a close neighbor to the Theater District. In keeping with the master plan's "Clean, Green and Grand" strategy, the district will receive numerous upgrades in paving, street lighting, street furniture and planting in addition to specific projects.

Seattle Theater District

The great Seattle World's Fair of 1964 left the city with the inheritance of the Seattle Center, an urban campus housing major landmarks such as the photogenic Space Needle and the International Fountain. The Fair also left the less auspicious legacy of a green heart surrounded by a hardened periphery that turns its back to important city thoroughfares. In GGN's new master plan for the north boundary of the original fair site, residual edge conditions that persist from the 1960s are reworked with a "Clean, Green, and Grand" theme. Central to the master plan are a combination of transformational strategies, including: establishment of a positive, proactive difference between daytime and nighttime environments; emphasis on a rhythm of buildings and spaces; a language of elements that includes lighting and signage to unify the street network. When implemented, the master plan will transform eight blocks of performance venues along busy Mercer Street (a major city arterial route) into a pedestrian-friendly corridor that links diverse contexts.

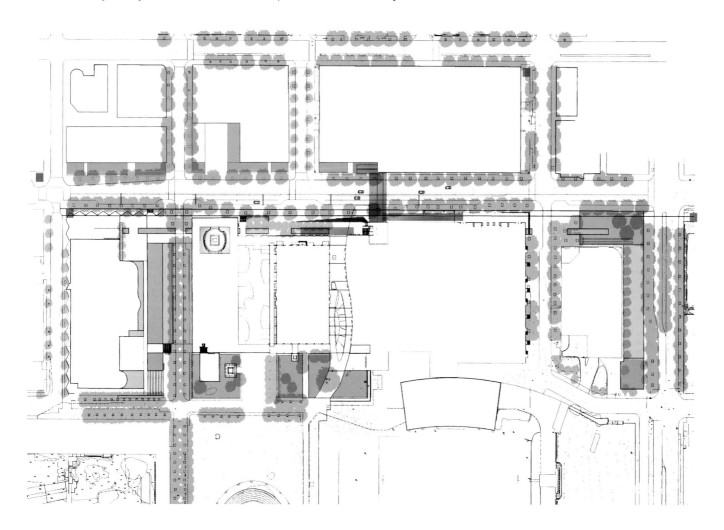

In the master plan, the daytime landscape of Mercer Street is unified by plantings and a linear water feature that frames separate entrances to five performance venues. The nighttime environment is transformed by Planes of Light using existing structures to cast dramatic illuminations on horizontal and vertical planes. The concept of variable atmospheric effects is based on emphasizing qualities appropriate to specific activities of day (business, education, and park access) and evening (theater promenade). Overall, the Theater District master plan unifies and enlivens the Mercer Street pedestrian environment with cohesive water elements, strategic plantings and glowing planes of color. At the same time, an historic miscue – the protected, inward orientation of the Seattle Center's open space – is pried open by articulation of interstitial passageways and incorporation of dissimilar architectural elements.

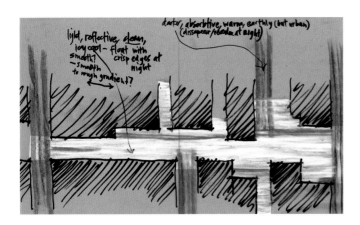

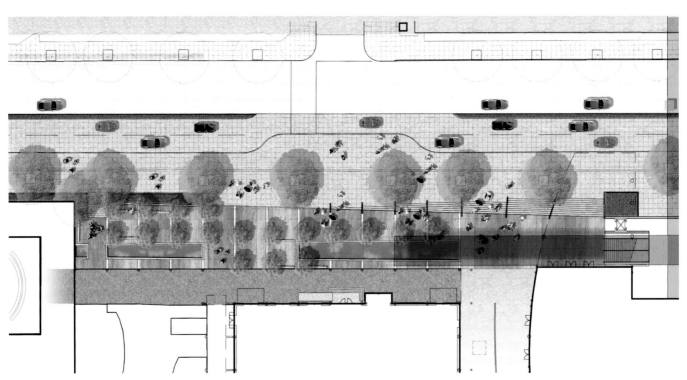

Lines of existing and new London Plane and other trees are proposed to reinforce the rhythm of urban form. Zones of turf and low plantings act as "Planes of Green" in crisp, orthogonal lines that complement the urban environment. Linear hedges of trimmed boxwood provide an east-west line of reference. Water features are proposed to link pedestrian areas and provide unique identities for individual locations. The existing architecture of the district is diverse, yet many locations share similar arts- and performance-oriented purposes. The master plan encourages venues to open their façades. Transparency between street and interior activities is expected to benefit the quality of the pedestrian experience by activating the shared places of everyday users and visitors.

Outside of its contract for the Theater District but in the spirit of the master plan, GGN won commissions to create site plans for Marion Oliver McCaw Hall and the Theater Commons. A green passageway into the Seattle Center campus, Theater Commons is tucked between the Seattle Repertory Theater and the Intiman Theater along Second Avenue. It is one of three entry points into the Seattle Center from the north. Like Kreielsheimer Promenade at McCaw Hall, the plaza acts as both a space of connection, of movement through, and a place of arrival, of pause.

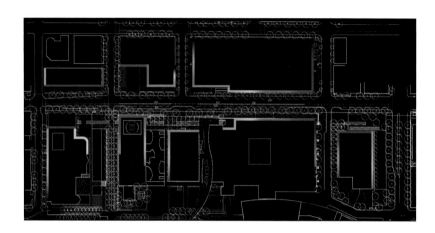

Bringing to life the master plan's "grand" aspect, Planes of Lights are designed to transform the Theater District with plays of light and color on both vertical and horizontal surfaces. Described as "light painting," saturated color washes on the ground plane, walls, canopies, columns and trees will redefine, distinguish and unify the atmospheric identities of venues and streetscapes at night (opposite page). Cooler colors are suggested for the periphery of the district, segueing to warmer hues of greater intensity toward the center. The overall lighting effects will be coordinated with each venue depending on architectural features and operating schedule (below).

Tension between rectilinear site proportions and the eloquent arc of the ground plane suggested by paving and water bodies (echoing the opera hall's façade) create an elongated curvature of space that pulls the eye from Mercer Street into the site, and beyond into the Seattle Center (from fore to distant ground – a favorite technique of Olmsted, among others).

Kreielsheimer Promenade and South Terrace at Marion Oliver McCaw Hall, Seattle

With minimal form and maximum effect, a plaza in Seattle wears the garments of multiple roles. A convenient, uncluttered urban passage by day, the Kreielsheimer Promenade carries pedestrians from busy Mercer Street into the heart of the Seattle Center campus. By night, the passage is illuminated with Planes of Light, a series of overhead metal scrims that glow in shades of white, hot reds, bright yellows, cool blues and hues between. Thin as a receding wave across smooth sand, three glistening sheets of water flow over sloped quartzite along the center of the space. The water magnifies the dark texture of stone below and reflects lively color from above.

Upon first approach, an apparently orthogonal volume opens between McCaw Hall and the Phelps Center. As one moves into and through the space, a gentle arc registers in the glass face of McCaw Hall.

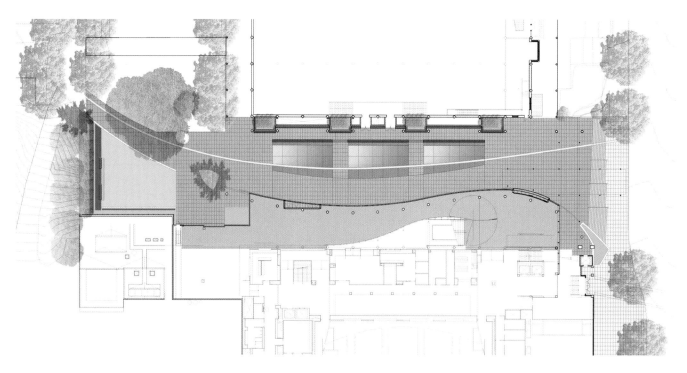

The arc is echoed more broadly on the horizontal plane by a curved seam of paving and again by the water's translucent lip as it spills into an inset band of a stainless steel grill. The generous radius of the promenade curvature is accentuated by line segments of stone bench that run parallel to the front of the Phelps Center. Viewed from the north, a cleanly framed glow of greenery draws the eye the length of the promenade to the South Terrace. Here an inclined patch of bounded lawn, a screen of climbing vines and a collection of magnificent, mature trees signal the segue from urban plaza to the parkland that surrounds the International Fountain. A legible connection is established between Mercer Street and the Seattle Center, areas otherwise too offset by grade and distance to sustain the sense of continuity so crucial to vital urban spaces.

With grandly-scaled features characterized by a simple clarity of materials, the promenade operates successfully as both an entry courtyard for the opera hall and a fully public, though hardly prosaic, pedestrian

The scheme is the first constructed evidence of the Theater District's strategic use of Planes of Light. Degrees of integration between interior and exterior volumes become most evident after dark, when dramatic lighting spills from inside and the spectacular Light Scrims (Leni Schwendinger Light Projects, Ltd.) glow outside, both captured by the water's reflection. Typical of contemporary urban projects, much of the plaza lies over mechanical systems and structure. It is subject to the constraints of a rooftop plaza: limited weight sectional space tolerances and difficult planting conditions. Dynamic water and lighting take the place of living materials, with the exception of four planted nooks along the Phelps Hall façade.

route. It also seems to work whether overflowing with crowds or providing moments of individual repose. As found in other Gustafson Guthrie Nichol projects, this is due to the provisional presence of light and water that underscores the site's atmospheric mutability. GGN is a champion of the city; its principals seem to realize that everyday ingredients such as pavement underfoot, street lighting and disjunctive spaces can be negotiated in a way that authenticate rather than obscure the urban experience.

Private Garden

A residential first for Gustafson Guthrie Nichol, this waterfront site proved an opportunity for the firm to modify strategies that it uses for larger, urban projects. How do ideas about scale, emptiness and fullness, molding plane tectonic into horizontal continuity change when applied to the interests of a single family? Shannon Nichol, lead designer, sees the scheme as typical of GGN's "expressively site-specific" process. The scheme is about site facts – both what is there and what's brought out by constructing land surface and movement – but also about what kinds of emotions and instincts emerge from contact with the land, its surroundings, and the residential architecture.

   Set on a lakeshore outside a major city, the site is simultaneously about embrace and outward push. A broken collar of hedge implies site boundaries by gathering and orienting spatial energies to the house

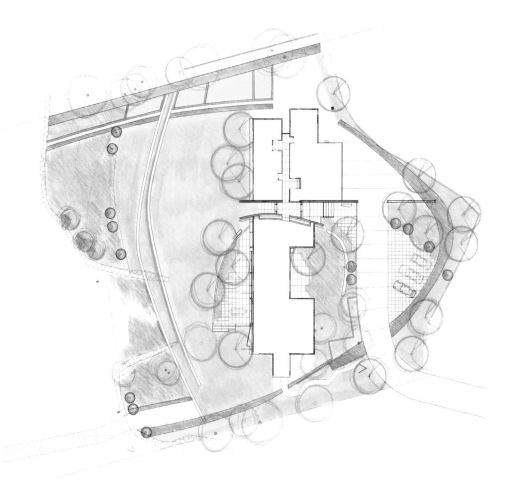

The collar hedge contains thuja and taxus evergreens. It is tallest at the base of the slope and is clipped progressively shorter toward the water's edge. The low, tapered, horizontal forms at the ends are similar in proportion to the land masses across the lake. Other plantings create a fusion of aromatic Mediterranean and coastal Pacific Northwest varieties that are woody, sculptural, and hardy. Existing picea and pinus topiary are retained and continue to be clipped into the pre-existing cloud-like forms in the Japanese tradition. Entry area plantings include warm colors and formal evergreens such as dwarf pines that presage the cloud topiary. The lake side features a cooler, lighter mix that appears translucent when back-lit by the sun setting over the water.

and lake. Green structure immediately engages visitors as the entry drive pierces and parking nests into the largest sweep of hedge. Moving outward from the residence, flush expanses of lawn and textured "horizon plantings" are interrupted by a grade shift at a wide retaining curve that pushes a convex face to the lake. This area creates the illusion of a wider horizon and foreshortens the water's edge so the distance to the water is reduced when viewed from the house. The goal is to bring the lake closer to the home while also emphasizing the sense that private land encompasses the residence. The dialog is not about extremes of inventiveness but about amplification derived from interpretation of place.

Diana, Princess of Wales Memorial Fountain, London

What happens when a memorial is laid down and occupied as an everyday space? Or when commemoration is not predicated upon a rationalized object – a solemn symbol of loss – but is about enabling subjective experience? "Reaching Out/Letting In," the title of Gustafson Porter's high-profile, passionately debated tribute to Diana, Princess of Wales, deviates from traditional memorials by offering an environment that is about joyfulness and reflection. The memorial can be visited and returned to many times for its qualities of open space, plantings, views and water. It is a landscape without frame that rests lightly alongside the Serpentine.

The core of the memorial is a fountain (as called for in the competition brief). Interpreted as necklace of water, the fountain is a horizontal element that flows downhill, hugging land form. The necklace accentuates an area of terrain without strictly defining its boundaries. Its embrace hints at a balance of two gestures:

Like a necklace tossed across an unwitting surface, placement of the water channel appears not to affect softly shaped contours that move through the interior. Undulating ground movements provide for seating, napping and viewing the Serpentine. From a distance, site contours blend into surrounding terrain (below). Aside from eight scattered trees and smoothly manicured turf, nothing occupies the encircled space but people. The result is an inclusive entity that is responsive to site, context, and the diversity of its public constituency without sacrificing self-definition as a bold, contemporary form. Originally molded by hand in clay, the fluid topography was then cast in resin to create a presentation model (below).

Water emits silently from a high point and descends in varying velocities and textures (or moods). The cascades meet in a shallow dished pool at the lowest point of the 0.4-hectare /over one-acre oval, closest to the Serpentine. Three bridges are provided across the channel allowing access to the oval's interior. The action of the water cascades is determined by the channel's topology: in cross section, profile and plan view, dimensions vary in depth and breadth. Digital imaging was used (opposite page) to model surface textures along each individual segment. The resin model was scanned to produce a 3D digital file, which was refined to create 542 digital files to computer-cut each piece of Cornish granite in Northern Ireland.

Diana was powerful, she reached out to affect those around her, but she also was vulnerable, and was impacted by what she let in.

The design and fabrication of the water channel are the result of advanced 3-D digital imaging and stone-cutting technology. Working in collaboration with the firms Barron Gould-Texxus and SDE, the designers modeled each segment of the granite channel individually and created full-size mock-ups of critical areas. Surface texture, edge configuration, channel profile and inclination vary, creating diverse water effects that bring out different moods as it glides, churns, rocks and bursts along the necklace before collecting in a shallow pool at the site's lowest point.

The simplicity of the water necklace is compelling because of its complex agenda. One finds a balance of assertion and vulnerability played out in the adaptivity of applied form to environment and in the

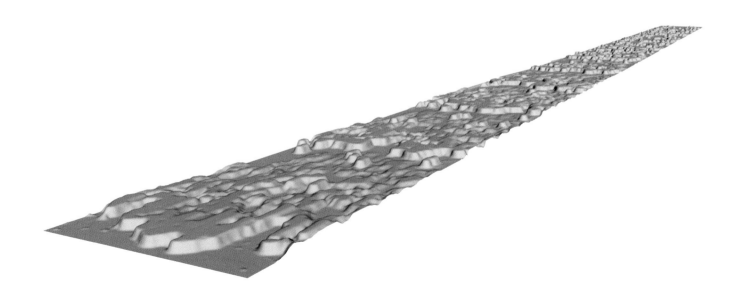

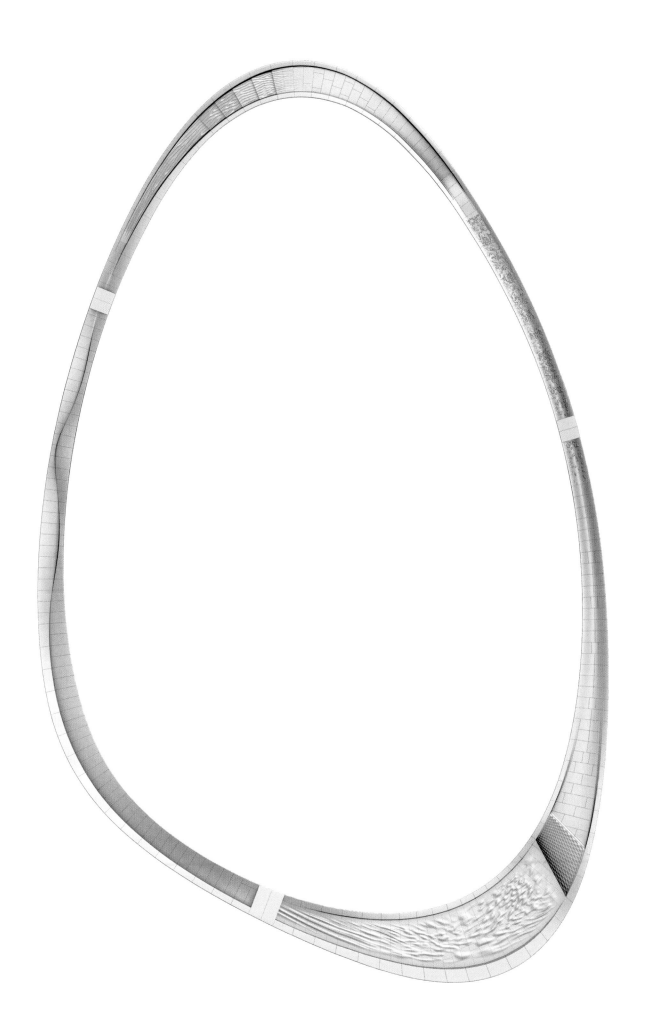

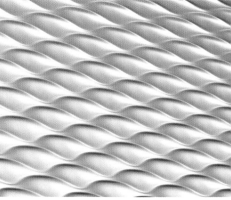

memorial's avoidance of didactic messages. "Reaching Out/Letting In" is a testament to the design team's take on Princess Diana but also to Gustafson and partners' habit of pairing unlike forces to generate concepts and forms. "Rational intuition," "complex simplicity," "force and fragility" are descriptors easily applied to the memorial scheme, also to a number of works in the firm's portfolio.

Framed Space

The wildly successful mix of giant bamboo varieties and tall mist pipes are refreshingly unconcerned with human scale. Outlined with Terrazzo, mosses and Soleirolia soleirolii/Helxine soleirolii (Baby's Tears) cover the ground plane. At the center is a shallow basin and inscribed arc of light (below and page 122). A pair of fountains contrasts "natural," slow overflow of water with "technical" high-speed water jets that first shoot horizontally over the natural and then mix with it. From the park, the glass-caged bamboo reads as an immense botanical specimen collected abroad in the tradition of explorers, presented in an industrially-scaled display (actual plants are from Prafrance Bambouseraie).

Parc de la Villette, Cité des Sciences et de l'Industrie Greenhouse, Paris

In an international competition won by Bernard Tschumi in the early 1980s, Parc de la Villette became a renowned example of theory translated into practice. A response to Kandinsky's study of point, line and plane and a treatise on deconstruction of the city, the creation of La Villette on the site of abandoned slaughter houses was greeted by critics unable to anticipate how the general public would use the unconventional arrangement of open spaces, follies, circulation and gardens. Set within the park, the Museum of Science, Technology and Industry, designed by the architect Adrien Fainsilber, was and remains an equally adventurous architectural construct. In the massive project's realization Kathryn Gustafson worked with the team responsible for the museum's façade of glass houses. Together with Ian Ritchie and Jacques Lemarque, the designer explored an age-old challenge that paralleled Tschumi's mating of abstraction and creation: the marriage of technology and nature.

Three *serres* (glass houses) extend off the south face of the museum, presenting ethereal glass cubes toward a sunken pool and the park's interior. RFR designed the *serre's* tension-supported glass structure (an innovation that today is commonly employed). Although all three were originally intended to house plantings, just one *serre* currently operates as a greenhouse. With the 300-meter square *serre* as site and La Villette as theoretical terrain, Gustafson's conceptual departure point was the transformation of nature by science. Allegories of this transformational energy materialize in the living media of plants, light and water. A visitor today sees a single *serre* bursting with a towering shock of bamboo seemingly appended to the museum. Far beyond expected dimensions, the scale of the *serre* and the vigor of the bamboo grove lead to thoughts of technologically enhanced growth that are exhilarating and menacing. Part Alice in Wonderland, part science experiment, the success of the single *serre* begs for its two companions to be activated.

Arthur Ross Terrace at the American Museum of Natural History, New York

The American Museum of Natural History has long played an important role in the cultural education of thousands of international visitors daily. In the 1990s, the museum and its grounds entered into a period of renovation and expansion. With the construction of the new Rose Center for Earth and Space by the Polshek Partnership, a limited competition for the adjacent terrace was held. The winning scheme by Kathryn Gustafson responds to the coming together of old and new within a conceptual framework of astronomy and the progression of science.

In Gustafson's reading, Polshek's floating sphere is an eclipsing lunar body. A conical silhouette is cast onto the ground, materializing into granite shadows that spill the length of the terrace, connecting the planetarium's contemporary glass box with the museum's venerable sandstone façade. An elongated trapezoid pierced by water jets, the moon shadow plaza ramps up slightly to accommodate the existing museum wing which is set

A paved plaza anchors the transparent cage housing the planetarium's grand sphere. Alternately bathed with water or featuring a dry paved surface, the tilted plane provides an activated visual surface when empty or a broad, open area for gatherings. Clean lines of stone and turf are enlivened with seasonal plantings that offer a degree of transition between the terrace's historic surrounds and its starkly contemporary neighbor. The primary east-west promenade along the site's northern edge (below, looking west) serves both as site circulation and as a wide, hardened lip that steps above a pre-existing slab to overlook Theodore Roosevelt Park. The promenade is called out by an allée of pagoda trees that will one day read as an architecturalized edge against the mixed woodland below.

higher than the finished floor elevation of the new planetarium. As the granite shadow stretches from the high-tech sphere to the stoop of the museum, a point is made that exploration and innovation evolve around established anchors of knowledge.

Light gray granite seating marks the major grade change between plaza and museum plinth. On the plinth, a double row of ginkgo trees parallels the museum's east face. The Ginkgo Balcony establishes a grounded entry area and reinforces two important site relationships: a pedestrian connection to Theodore Roosevelt Park via stairs to the north, and framed views back to the planetarium, visually linking old to new. Wide-paved corridors carry daily foot traffic along both sides of the terrace.

Within its urban configuration of plaza, promenade, balcony and plantings, the Ross Terrace offers a story specific to natural history and astronomy studies. But like the Rose Center, the terrace stands at odds with its

The central plaza is washed with a scrim of water one quarter-inch deep, allowing the space to take on a reflective sheen that meets and intensifies the planetarium's glowing glass sheath. Via comet trails etched into the plaza surface, water is collected and carried to a shallow pool at the base of the glass enclosure. Jets and fiber-optic lights set within the plane suggest the constellation Orion. The jets and water scrim can operate separately, simultaneously or be turned off for social gatherings (anchored tent ties allow the entire central space to be covered during inclement weather). Throughout the terrace, strategic lighting illuminates the space into a nighttime spectacle.

traditionally-styled physical surrounds. The terrace presents a well-defined structure and refinement of sensory experiences (focused illumination, degrees of reflectivity, constant and ephemeral textures) that are typical of Gustafson and partners' "Framed Spaces." This is in contrast to the general appeal of pastoral leafiness found in the nearby park. The Ross Terrace is a moment of imagination trained with vitalizing clarity beyond the immediate locale.

Great Glass House Interior, National Botanic Garden of Wales

In a contemporary take on the Victorian Age glass house, there sits in south Wales a dramatic glass hall that displays Mediterranean plants from five continents. Sir Norman Foster's 100-meter long, single-span dome is a sky that soars over a rugged terrain designed by Gustafson Porter. At first glance, the context, the site and the client's program might seem to be paradoxically at odds with one another. Extremes of climate and topography are required to create appropriate environments for a broad-ranging palette of endangered plants, yet Foster's glass dome (the site) provides an expanse of undifferentiated enclosure rising out of temperate pasture land. The solution? A variety of microclimates are created by shaping the ground plane into various degrees of protection, exposure, moisture and aridity. The results include high cliffs, a steep-sided ravine and stepped, stacked terraces: spaces and conditions inspired by natural systems but functioning as sculptural forms that support cultural display.

Sir Norman Foster's Great Glass House rises out of the Welsh countryside, its rounded form surprisingly at ease with the surrounding topography (opposite page). Inside the glass dome, quite the opposite occurs: a ruggedly angular, semi-arid landscape of cliffs, ravines and terraces presents a startling contrast to the region's verdant patchwork. An early concept sketch (below, above left) and a schematic section (below, above right) depict the prominent role played by what might appear to be constructed landform. Instead, the dramatic contours are created by carving down into existing grade beneath the dome. The botanic garden plantings have fared well in the artificial environment.

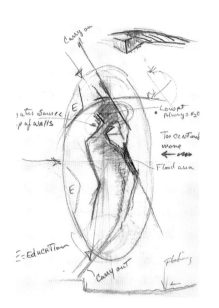

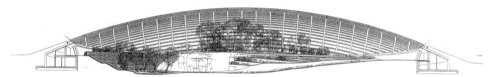

 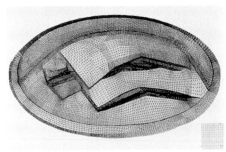 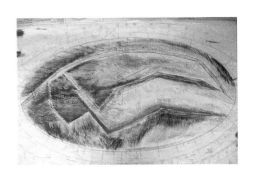

Images at the top of the opposite page reveal aspects of Gustafson and partners' design process. Ideas are worked out initially as quick, diagrammatic sketches which gain more clarity over time.

With the primary concepts agreed upon, a clay model is created that then is cast in plaster for presentation. Notably absent at these stages are surface articulations, such as paving textures, and planting information. In the botanic garden (below and opposite page, bottom, photographs taken just after preliminary installation of materials), visitors interact with the land forms and have the option to pick their own routes across crushed gravel scree surfaces. In the designers' words, "multiple horizons and over-lapping routes stretch the scale of the space."

The garden's topography was achieved not by adding earth to the floor of the glass house to build up contours, but by pushing down into the earth and carving out real ground. Plant collections grow not on artificial surfaces but primarily on armatures of solid earth and rock. As visitors explore the garden, they pass through continually changing spaces, discovering differing effects of growth, moisture, light and shadow. A channel cuts roughly across the center of the Great Glass House, descending to a depth of five meters in a narrow space that squeezes between two rough cliff faces. Visitors are brought into close proximity with chiseled stone and textural plant life. The terrain forces a type of first hand experience unlike conventional, framed exhibits set apart from curious eyes. The circulation scheme gives visitors choices and requires active participation. Numerous paths introduce horizon lines that fluctuate between the panoramic and the subterranean. In a deviation from the standard method of prescribed circuit, here the crushed gravel scree

surface allows people to wander off primary routes in search of their own points of interest. Importantly, positioning of the body relative to land form and sunlight controls individual perspectives, although one never escapes the immense scale of the dome.

Throughout the garden, irrigation water interacts with the idiosyncrasies of topography in an informal and seemingly organic manner as opposed to an engineered, scheduled, mechanistic delivery. Water seeps, trickles and cascades over cliff faces, through zones of periodic flooding, into circulating and stagnant pools. Soil type, degrees of inundation and angle of exposure to the sun that penetrates the glass dome provide a calculated matrix of nutritional determinants that bring to life year-round patterns of color, density and texture. Unlike traditional botanical displays that focus on blooms and foliage, this garden is strategically designed to feature dormant and productive phases with equal emphasis. Plant groupings are composed to

Excavated earth forms are faced in rough sandstone that showcases light/shadow effects as well as surface texture caused by plant growth and water action (below). A high, narrow gorge creates a spatial experience that is enhanced by moving water spilling down vertical rock buttresses, flowing under and alongside pathways (opposite page). Water emerges silently from specific source points, washes over stone, and is collected by a shallow lake formed by stone slabs. Universal access is provided along a gabion wall at the garden's south side (opposite page, right, distant ground). Fences and handrails are avoided when possible; where needed, they are pulled away from the wall face to distinguish the "natural" from the manmade.

allow the decline of one species's output to complement or visually inform the growth cycle of another. All species are native to the Mediterranean region and propagated from seeds or plants taken at the site of origin. Rather than propose a definitive planting plan, the designers created a template of colors and heights into which the lead horticulturalist designated plants to fulfill the design criteria (the garden's initial installation plan, in which low-growing, yellow-green plants rose up to densely planted, silver-greens and then came down to mid-sized, dark greens as one moved into and above the ravine, was directed by Ivor Stokes). Beauty, the aesthetic of conventional floral garden display, ceases to be a mandate and is replaced by the provision of sensory stimuli.

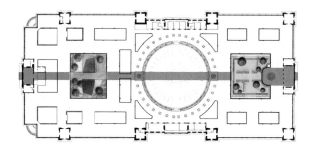

Courtyards, Government Offices Great George Street, London

In the heart of London, Whitehall is dense with governmental organizations whose spaces have gained potent cultural associations over time. While some are preserved as historical showcases (the War Rooms, for example), others continue to be important to governmental operations and require updating to conform with contemporary functions. With the renovation and expansion of H. M. Treasury, Gustafson Porter was commissioned to redesign a pair of courtyards that flank the central interior court (simultaneously under reconstruction by architects Foster and Partners). Set on axis between St. James Park and Whitehall, the courtyards occupy roughly square volumes that once served as light wells. Fraternal twins emerging consecutively from the design dialog of Gustafson Porter (schematics for the West Courtyard were completed before the office received the commission for the East), the spaces share familial traits such as an underlying cruciform structure but have independent internal orders that differ in response to unique site conditions.

Along the West Courtyard walkway, flanking shallow dishes are pressed down into the ground plane to form a hybrid of natural pool and engineered water work. Water has a figural presence and occupies as opposed to structures space; its quiet glisten contrasts the matt finish of the courtyard slate. Along the edge of the walk, a thin wood bar, smoothly sculpted and set on steel, provides a handrail that doubles as a bench to perch upon lightly. The East Courtyard offers intimate gardens within a modern interpretation of the formal parterre. Evergreen-clipped hedges frame the principal route and outdoor rooms. Hedge heights restrict and reveal views of various garden spaces.

Within each courtyard, the cross-axial armature is softened by gentle manipulation of the ground plane in plan and section. The resulting *bas relief* presents a thickened, figural horizontality that allows subtle separation from the surrounding architecture.

In the West Courtyard the sectional interplay (first explored via a cut-and-fold diagram faxed from Porter to Gustafson) is about hardened land form that reveals an equilibrium of forces at work. While the paved ground plane gently pushes up into a causeway which arcs horizontally and vertically along the central axis, a perpendicular motion depresses the courtyard surface.

Water appears to slip beneath the causeway but it is held apart in two bodies created when the original elevation was simultaneously depressed and raised to express cross axes. The sectional difference exposes a contrasting material like the satin lining of a pin-striped suit. The dished pools can be drained for gatherings.

A lighting trench along the courtyard's perimeter emphasizes the transition between interior and exterior. The East Courtyard is broken into subspaces by sculptural hedges. Planted 240 millimeters below but with tops clipped to, the arc of the walkway surface, yew and boxwood segments frame views and create a center high point at the intersection of the cruciform. From the primary path, it is not possible to read the true base of the hedge lines and from below, the green walls move just above and below eye level. Arranged to accommodate a stairwell, a café and an adjacent library, the courtyard's four quadrants contain perennials, ferns and bulbs that bring seasonal highlights to the evergreen framework. Plants are arranged in bands with mixes organized according to height, leaf shape and texture. A narrow rill of moving water runs along three of the courtyard's four sides. Unlike the bold, planar presence of water in the West Courtyard, here water is a perimeter element that brings atmospheric effects.

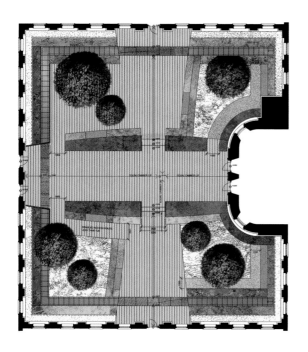

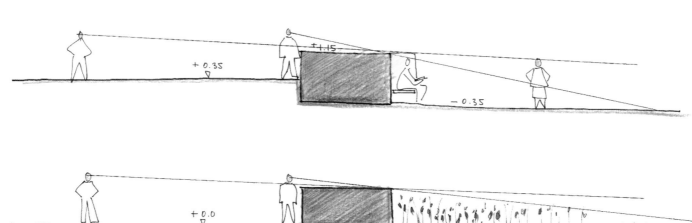

Both courtyards are used by Treasury and Customs Excise and Inland Revenue employees. The courtyards are conceived as a pair with direct conceptual links. Given the shady conditions, Gustafson Porter concluded that the best chance of successful plantings would be to create a woodland quality that would evolve into a full green matt with leafy canopy above. Trees were craned over the top of the Treasury walls and dropped into place. All plants are chosen to extend the flowering season, with blooms from early spring through autumn. In the West Courtyard, plantings are primarily blue and white. The flower color in the East Courtyard ranges from white to blue, mid-pink and purple.

Art Institute of Chicago, New North Wing Courtyard and Streetscape

Situated between Michigan Avenue and Grant Park, the Art Institute of Chicago offers Neoclassical architecture in harmony with its surrounds. A collection of small urban gardens are tucked into the corners of the Institute. Without confronting the museum's dominant character, the gardens each represent the era of their making. For example, while being modern in inspiration, the South Garden by Dan Kiley has a geometry and structural clarity that dovetails with the adjacent Beaux-arts façades. With the construction of Renzo Piano's new north wing there is an interest in establishing a contemporary cultural dialog with the newly opened, neighboring Millennium Park – a dialog potentially as seminal as the Institute's original relationship with Grant Park. GGN designed a courtyard and streetscape tucked alongside the new addition that relate to the wing's clean lines, open volumes and its Asian collections. The courtyard, visible through the gallery's glass curtain walls from Monroe Street, is one of three primary areas: the Monroe streetscape,

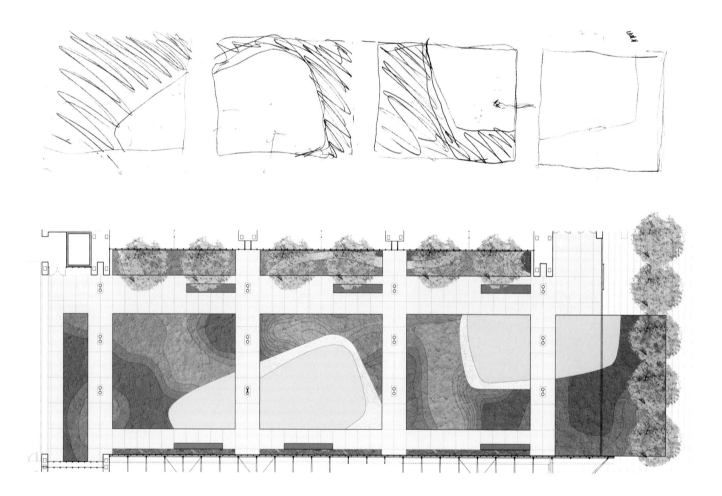

The assertive, punched-up ground plane responds to the scale of the courtyard's open volume (185 feet long by 65 wide and 65 high). The Mod Pod groupings are a mix of four hedge types that range in height from 12 to 48 inches. Growth is shaped by a metal clipping guide composed of vertical poles spaced on a three-foot grid. To force perspective, coarse-leafed varieties are used on the east and west ends of the courtyard with fine textures at the center. Narrow paths between plantings provide maintenance access for hand clipping without detracting from the sense of coherent horizontality and movement. Accent plantings line the inside face of carved-out areas.

the Columbus streetscape, and the courtyard. The governing device of the courtyard is horizontal mass created by tightly grouped, clipped shrubs. Initially inspired by Asian art screens, lithographs and calligraphy, the rise and fall of the vegetal plane defines the area's spatiality. The undulating massings, or "Mod Pods" (modular pods) serve as a backdrop for the museum's extensive Asian art collection. The form is meant to read as one mass that is broken at the building column lines and carved out in the pod areas. "The Mod Pods' horizontal muscle corresponds to the building's interior voids," says Jennifer Guthrie. "The courtyard is a substantial space that needs a strong horizontal component to ground it and to preserve the experience of expansiveness." Within the contoured hedge volumes, two large gathering areas are carved out. Shaped intuitively by hand in sketch and model, the open zones will be surfaced in grass and hardy ground covers. Ginkgo trees extend across the Mod Pods' eastern limit to connect with the streetscapes and a drop-off area.

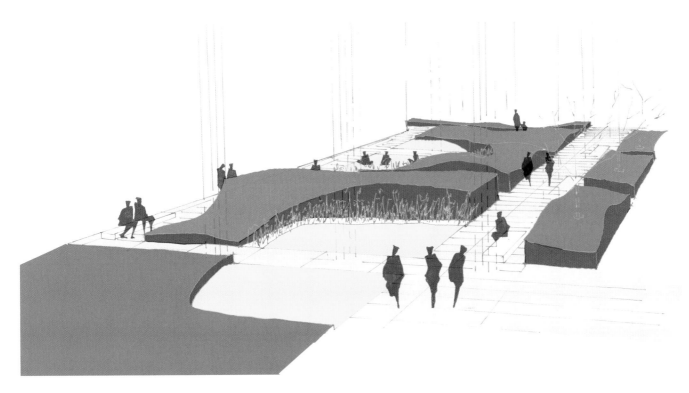

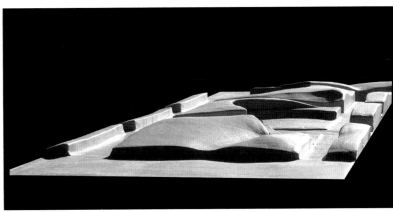

Places of Translation

Gardens of the Imagination, Terrasson

The idea of the garden as a lure is ancient. Although the tradition had more to do with pilgrimage or politics than entertainment, the destination garden as a place of enrichment and sensory experience is present in many cultures throughout time. Thus when Terrasson, deep in the Perigord region, came up with the idea to build a garden composed of a number of smaller gardens, each representing historic types from around the world, the small town was not making history in the cultural sense yet was hoping to literally *make* history with a series of experiential, interpretative installations in which elements of traditional gardens are translated into contemporary form.

In the initial project competition, a scheme entitled "Fragments of the History of Gardens" was produced by a collaborative team of landscape architects, artists, garden historians and architects headed by Kathryn Gustafson and members of Paysage Land. Although the selective interpretation of historic models is

Water is a guiding element throughout the garden. A narrow channel parallels the walk that ascends from the village to the garden gates (below left). A dense bank of boxwood along the woodland walk is punctuated by shingled Water Stairs that carry glistening trickles from above (below right and opposite page). Only later in the garden circuit is the origin of the water discovered. In the Elements Garden – the first in the history fragments sequence – a gold ribbon of anodized aluminum weaves through the trees just above eye level (page 145). Beneath the ribbon, four small gardens explore the transformation of native plants through hybridization (including rhododendron/azalea, Montpelier maple, ferns, and mosses).

inherently a didactic process, it's clear that rediscovery rather than re-presentation was the goal of the creative team. If one looks beyond the common, current usage of didacticism as pedagogic or moral instruction to its Greek roots in the relaying of information as well as pleasure, the team's design process is clarified. What reads most strongly and persists most richly after a visit to Terrasson are the sensations borne from the siting of pieces such that a new, nearly feral *genus loci* is established for each garden fragment. Light, sound, movement, color, fragrance, spatial depth and texture resonate within each installation, bringing forth defining characteristics that have more to do with intuitive imprinting than rational reference points. It's this phenomenon that lends itself readily to the scheme's eventual renaming and subsequent marketing hook, "Gardens of the Imagination."

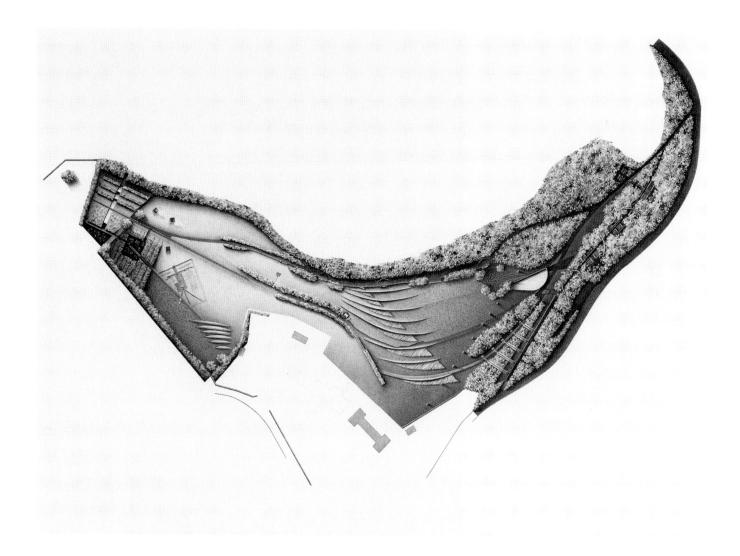

On the opposite page at top, the Elements Garden encompasses visitors with a combination of airy native woodland and engineered plantings. A pergola marks the entrance into the Elements Garden (opposite page, bottom). In plan view (page 144), the history fragments sequence moves roughly counterclockwise from the lower right corner, with the Perspective marking the center of the site. The Perspective is a land movement piece, a *trompe l'oeil* of grasses, white roses and blue perennials that engages the eye both from the town below and looking out from the height of the garden (pages 155, 156 and 157). The Water Garden is located at the far left of the site plan, the Rose Garden adjacent at its lower right.

Throughout the garden, elements are located according to pre-existing site features and are informed by dramatic topography. Spread over a 25-percent north-facing slope overlooking the village and the Vézère River valley, the *pentimenti* of an old drainage system and cistern wells underlay woodland floors and meadow grasses. Cliffs pocked with caves define the top edge of the site. A mature oak forest spills downward from the cliffs into open fields and mixed stands of oak, acacia and maple. The design scheme lacks an explicit superstructure; instead, individual episodes relate closely to specific microconditions. Natural occurrences are in some cases barely distinguishable from inserted architecture, such as the juxtaposition of Ian Ritchie's gabion-walled, passive solar *serre* below a grass and steel amphitheater. The glass roof of the *serre* hovers, reflective as a small lake at the forested edge. Existing trees punctuate and pierce the theater's iconic, stepped form. Elsewhere, native species are displayed alongside hybridized

varieties, blurring the distinction between nature and cultivated botanical display. Throughout, plants and water can appear in their native condition of forest, meadow and brook, as well as in the productive vernacular of woodland, terraced bed, allée, arbor, cistern and irrigation channel. In some areas, existing material is simply edited, as in the mossy, rock-littered forest floor beneath the cliffs. More than 5,000 trees, shrubs and perennial plants are used to create formal elements, narrative chapters, sequenced views and the occasional forced perspective to evoke historic garden technique.

The garden speaks in lines of sight that are fusions of traditional and contemporary techniques of controlling perception. Discovery of vistas located along the circuit is an activity, much like in the landscape gardens of the Romantic era. In place of allegorical reference points that require knowledge transferred from literature, history and art to participate, however, all that is required here is receptivity to sensation.

Upon leaving the Elements Garden, visitors discover Ian Ritchie's elegantly minimal *Serre* (below, top right and opposite page). A gabion-walled structure capped by a floating glass roof, the *Serre* operates on passive energy and houses exhibition space, a café and bookstore. Next to the *Serre*, molded land set with steel arcs and steps serves as a boldly simple amphitheater looking over the village and beyond (below, bottom). Continuing along the circuit, one encounters the back of the Perspective land waves. Various incarnations of woodland make reference to wilderness, to productive land, to cultured nature (moss garden below, left). Remnants of the site's agricultural past are incorporated, including cisterns, terracing and water conduits.

Activation of the senses to spark imagination is the end game, not the transfer of knowledge from designer to audience. Control is relinquished and the audience is free to apply their own cultural and personal associations. One guesses that a western European visitor might have a different take on the gardens than an Asian audience, that a family with young children categorizes the experience in a different way than a retired urban couple.

As one traverses the slope from tightly packed, light-filtered woods to prominent exposure, from intimate rooms splashed with water through vivid plantings and along axial thrusts, changes in ground surface often call out arrival into a garden fragment. What the foot touches upon and where the eye rests coalesce at times to tether focal perception to immediate surroundings. At other times, the two peel away from each other, the eye draws upward and outward, off site while the feet remain *in situ*. Within each vignette, the framing

Organized in a traditional cruciform, the Water Garden features several garden cultures, including Persian, Mogul, Egyptian, and Renaissance (these pages and page 152 and 154). Framed by willow trees and shrubs, the room of water has a paved floor set with a random grid of water jets. The floor is bisected by a channel that flows from a cascade above through planted terraces into a broad pool below. In the lower pool fifteen randomly spaced sprinklers emit sprays that refract sunlight, making translucent rainbows (page 152). The sequence can be understood as a progression of water uses, from irrigation to pleasure to embellishment.

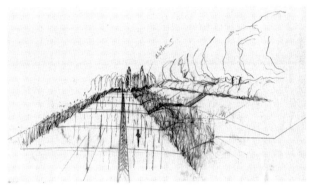

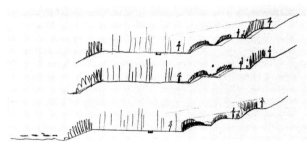

In the Rose Garden (below), a 1,000-square-meter steel structure negotiates the sloping hillside to support a tapestry of roses. The palette of climbing varieties describes a history of the flower while providing an optical transition of from pale to intensely saturated coloration. In season, the impact of the roses' collective fragrance is a powerful experience that, like the sounds of lively water, momentarily disengages the eye and allows an alternate sense to dominate. Below the Rose Garden, near the slope's base, slivered basins set into the grade represent the practice of collection and retention of water – agriculture's most precious resource.

A second water channel flows west from the Water Garden. As the hillside steepens, the stepped channel becomes a retaining wall that pulls the eye laterally across the site's center (opposite page).

Continuing along the circuit, from the Pathway of Fountains a vaulted allée leads to the Topiary Room (page 147). The pathway then traces the toe of a perspective land wave (below, bottom) before reaching the end of the garden circuit at the Sacred Forest, an existing oak grove with a clearing of field grasses and wildflowers (below, top right). Fifty bells suspended in the oak trees enliven the space and set it apart from adjacent oak stands.

of views can shift from close-enough-to-touch foreground to hazy distance. The contrast of the tangible very-near (grooved trunks, massed blossoms, waving grasses, weathered rock, water in motion) and the unattainable far-away undermines the coherency of the site's message. You're not here, it says. You're in a place that exists physically but which is assimilated and afterwards resides in the space of the imagination. It is up to you to locate the pieces, to corroborate sensation and information.

One leaves the Gardens of the Imagination with a vague sense of having learned something, or having refound a lost memory. Lacking interpretive signage, the garden installations evoke whimsy anchored by the dignity of historic reference. Terrasson titillates, and one realizes how rarely sustained stimulation of the senses occurs. Perhaps discovery of this is true learning.

Five carved stone tablets rest on the earth within the Sacred Forest, each inscribed with a plan view of a major river delta of the world (below, top right). Water is carried in the delta incisions, feeding the Water Stairs that spill down alongside the garden's entry walk. From the village, visitors see the Perspective land forms (opposite page and below) and the Axis of the Wind, a line of wind vanes climbing the hill above town (below, bottom). The wind vanes are twelve meters high and have an articulated joint that allows the piece to orient according to the wind's direction as well as its vertical drafts. Each mast holds a bell that chimes in heavy winds.

Court of Appeals Courtyard, Aix-en-Provence

Along historic Cours Mirabeau, the central artery of Aix-en-Provence, one comes to the Palace of Justice area within the city's old town. Originally the site of royal gardens, the district gained its current layout in the late 18th century during a phase of urban renewal directed by city leaders and paid for by wealthy merchants. In the process, a prison was transformed into the Aix-en-Provence Court of Appeals. Two hundred years later, Kathryn Gustafson reworked the building's courtyard to tell a story about site history. Taking clues from existing artifacts, the courtyard expresses layers of time in water, stone and metal.

    The oldest, or deepest, layer present is rocks from a 12th century nouria. A type of well featuring a wood water wheel with terra-cotta pots, the town nouria once served as a central public space in the medieval era. Exactly as discovered during the construction, the nouria stones are loosely arranged in an oval that corresponds to the old well location. The second layer of site history is the stone block foundation of André

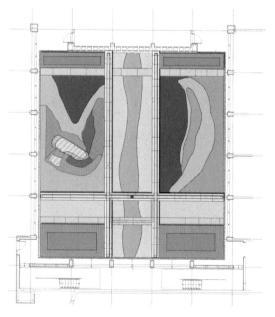

When construction began on the new Court of Appeals, it was expected that remains of Ledoux's building foundations would be uncovered. Unexpected was the discovery of the nouria's much older urban form. Both the Ledoux foundation pieces and the well remnants were recorded and removed by archeologists during construction. The foundation was replaced and the nouria reconstructed in the exact location and elevation as they had been found. Like *pentimenti* on a master painter's canvas, old lines reveal the layered site history of this sector of Aix-en-Provence. In the detail image below, the overlapping stories become a material expression of stone, steel and water.

Ledoux's original buildings. Classical in its bilateral symmetry and cross axes, the partial foundation gives the courtyard garden a compositional armature against which less regular figures are read.

The third layer represents Gustafson's current-day involvement in the evolution of the courtyard. Wanting to bring moving water back into the site, the designer set steel edging on Ledoux's foundation blocks to create narrow channels. Steel segments inserted into the channel interact with the water flow, setting up partial weirs that vary water patterns and sound. The metal is intended to be a strong presence but to sit lightly within the venerable foundation stones. Mosses and ferns are planted on the courtyard's often shaded open surfaces. Primarily a visual feature, the design scheme offers an allegory of justice moving with transparency in a slow, linear fashion bounded by the strictures of an inherited system.

South Coast Plaza Bridge and Strata Garden, Costa Mesa

In the 1980s, developer C. J. Segerstrom broke new ground for upscale commercial environments when he commissioned Isamu Noguchi to create "California Scenario" in a 1.6-acre courtyard of the South Coast performing arts and financial development area. Nearly two decades later, Kathryn Gustafson and collaborators were hired by the Segerstroms to design a pedestrian bridge and garden plaza in the shopping complex. Both projects are concerned with the history of Southern California's landscape. Noguchi's acclaimed work is an arrangement of sculpted forms that create sceneography reminiscent of regional land types. In terms of form and narrative, Gustafson's scheme is a more deeply abstracted and personalized interpretation of the role water, earth forces and population growth play in the arid region. Designed in collaboration with James Poulson of Ellerbe Becket Architects, Gustafson's bridge scheme links South Coast Plaza to Crystal Court by lofting a 600-foot-long bougainvillea-draped steel structure over existing roads

The dominant concept behind the design of the 600-foot-long bridge is a bird in flight (below right). At nearly twenty feet wide, the bridge is closer in type to a civic promenade than a utilitarian access route (below). The structure's delicate ribs support the deck and overhead panels that arc gracefully over parking and roadways. Steel outriggers extend forty feet out from the bridge deck with beams tapered to give an impression of aerodynamic uplift (page 162). Alternating with the long outriggers, shorter beams provide additional support for steel cables that run the length of the bridge. The cables create an arbor planted with purple and pink bougainvillea.

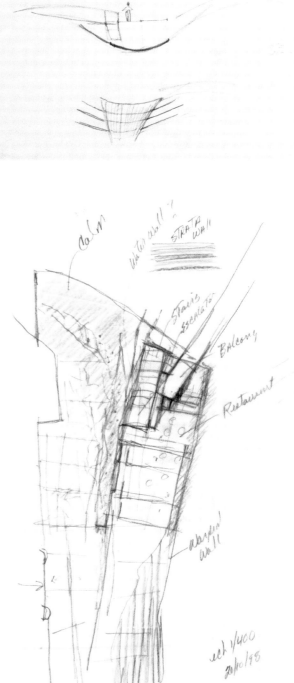

The paired images below feature a plaster model of the design scheme (left) and a computer-generated collage layered on top of a photograph of existing conditions (right). The plaster model succinctly illustrates the scheme's Slip Plates. The plates represent movement at both human and geologic scales that is a cause and result of pressures building over time. The digital rendering shows the colored strata of the terrace, revealing shifting planes that overlap. Plant materials include eucalyptus along the south elevation, jacaranda trees as a western terminus and focal point, boxwood and flowering shrubs. In the upper right corner of the collage, the end of the bridge is visible with its wings of bougainvillea.

and parking. The bridge touches down on a garden plaza that for the most part eschews horticultural materials for a geologic parti. Plates replace plots, fault lines are sinuous site and sight axes, and an enlarged sense of time and motion emerges.

Geology is primarily about time. It is also, inexorably, about movement. Incremental or immense, over years or in a sudden moment, change occurs. In the Strata Garden, the designers use this conceptual foundation as a metaphor for human nature in constant flux. Tension builds; plates slip, release, and return temporarily to a stable state. Along the length of the plaza, five parallel planes of colored stone alternately uplift and weigh down, reveal and constrain, accumulate and shed pressure. The stone bands portray plate tectonics but also refer to the constant push of immigration and population growth that each year moves development farther into Southern California's open lands. Breaks in the stratified ground plane do not

come as a surprise but are difficult to anticipate, as are events in life, due to their non-regular occurrence. Where breaks occur, bold layers of stone appear in section. The reductive rhythm brings into prominence water flow, sunlight and shadow that heighten the experiential impact of the garden.

Rising from the plaza's spine, a grand stair condenses the motion of the garden's plates into steps that ascend to meet the eastern end of the pedestrian bridge. When materials underfoot change from stone to steel, the bridge begins its curving sweep toward Crystal Court. Generously proportioned with a fourteen-foot-wide deck of post-tensioned concrete, the bridge is wrapped in dimpled, perforated stainless steel panels. Extending tapered steel beams on twenty-foot intervals, the structure takes flight with fluid calm. The bridge arcs gently in plan and, as it nears the garden plaza, in section, giving pedestrians an overlook that cantilevers slightly above the Strata Garden. Inspired by the evolution of Southern California from an

Principal garden materials are stone and water. Stone is layered in parallel strata of muted colors that represent the geologic history of the site. Water rises from bubbling pools, to evoke the region's hot springs and agricultural heritage, then cuts through the planar rock to collect in channels and pools for distribution.

arid ecosystem to irrigated, cultivated lands to intense (sub)urban development, air, reminiscent of the regional hot springs, bubbles up into two pools and feeds a narrow fissure carved into the stepped ground plane. As water is conveyed and eventually consumed or consummated by return to the earth, references are made to exploited resources such as oil, precious metals and water. Given the mixed message of consumerism (upscale mall) and ambitious cultural precedent (Noguchi's acclaimed installation), the bridge and Strata Garden mediate well. The plaza provides needed functionality (access to parking, improved connectivity between commercial areas, café space) within the conceptual framing of geography, geomorphology and emotional realignment.

"Wind, Sound and Movement" – SF MoMA Exhibition

In 2001, the San Francisco Museum of Modern Art presented "Revelatory Landscapes," five site-specific installations by West Coast-based teams of landscape architects and artists. Described in one review as a show about revealing "hidden aspects of the land," the projects offered new ways to experience *terrains vagues*, the interstitial spaces of the city. By their very nature of being ever present, many aspects of our daily landscapes do not register on the occupied brain. The exhibition schemes provided devices that encouraged visitors to momentarily readjust cultural periscopes, to experience alternate perceptions of urban spaces, to find profundity in the prosaic.

Located above the south bay on Candlestick Point Hill, the site was selected by Gustafson and design collaborator Jaimi Baer and was fully exposed and wind-swept. Partially scarred by construction of Candlestick land fill, the site had three areas to which the scheme responded: first, a seemingly undisturbed

The temporary installation spoke about how the city's natural and cultural landscape effect one another as disturbed sites undergo changes wrought by natural phenomena such as wind, water and volunteer plant communities (opposite page). Remnants of terracing gave the slope a sense of abandonment that alluded to an urban or industrial past. Over time, the disturbed earth was covered by dense overgrowth of successional and invasive species, such as pampas grass, whose seeds were carried by shoreline winds. Spinners set into the grass tufts rendered the invisible shape of the wind visible by marking the pattern of seed distribution and by moving with the speed and direction of daily winds (below).

upper hillside with a mix of volunteers and plants installed for erosion control; second, a terraced slope with an assortment of native, introduced and invasive species; third, a flat plateau with primarily invasive species indicative of disturbed sites (such as pampas grass). The design brought focus to the soil disturbance caused by the terracing and the resulting spread of wind-deposited pampas grass seeds.

Upon approach to the site, wind chimes greeted visitors and alerted the ear to the movement of winds across the installation area. 300 spiraled mylar spinners placed in pampas grass clumps caught the eye and relayed information about how wind patterns scattered seeds over the terrain. On the plateau, a collection of Sound Chairs provided places to sit to take in the symbiosis of artificial and natural landscape forces. Fabricated with three-foot-diameter corrugated pipe, the curvature of the chair backs reduced highway noise and amplified site sounds. Wind and its powers of sound and movement are phenomena that play

To access the installation, visitors followed a grass track ascending west from Candlestick Stadium (opposite page, left). After several hundred feet, one encountered an "aural entry point" where wind chimes were heard. Interspersed with hundreds of spinners and wind chimes, a collection Sound Chairs welcomed visitors (below, left). Information about the site's history was stenciled on the back of the chairs. In contrast to the air traffic overhead and nearby Highway 101, the chairs offered an invitation to pause, to experience the movement, sound and long-term effects of the wind. Without the proximity of urban intensity, revelation of the site's natural phenomena would not have been as effective.

leading roles in several Gustafson projects. According to the designer, wind is "a force that can be perceived through the environment" via design elements that heighten awareness of its effects on specific geographies. In this installation, the fact that wind has and continues (despite urban expansion) to shape the city's topographical and vegetal matter is a revelation that can be applied to numerous sites around the Bay Area.

Crystal Palace Park, London

In describing their approach to the rehabilitation of the historic Crystal Palace park grounds, Kathryn Gustafson and Neil Porter use phrases such as "an overwhelming feeling of lost place," "a past dream," and later, when it became clear that just a portion of their original 53-hectare proposal would be funded, "heartbreaking." This depth of emotional connection to a site is unusual but is merited by the chasm between the park's eminent past and its modern day exploitation. The Crystal Palace, designed by Joseph Paxton, was celebrated as an architectural wonder before its destruction in 1936. Subsequently the grounds – laid out as an early example of a city park in the iconoclastic English landscape garden style – were subjected to neglect and in some areas, development.

Working with the architect John Lyall, Gustafson Porter's initial site analysis identifies two elements that give the park its identity. One is Paxton's grand formal terraces, in places bulging and crumbling from poor

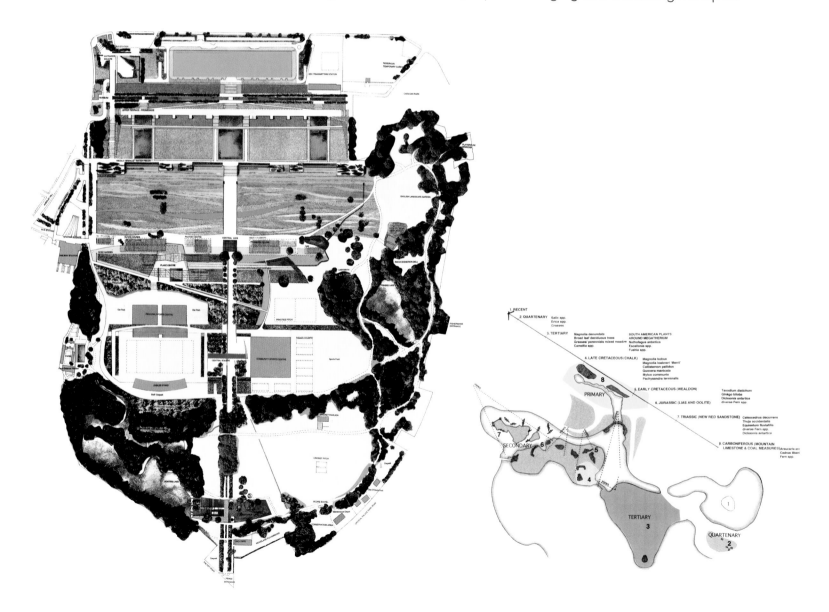

Gustafson Porter's original proposal (opposite page, left) features a lateral grid of sorts applied over the historic main axis, allowing for future-phased development to occur in a spatially organized manner. The scheme revives and reinvents the monumental palace terraces and envisions new gardens, rippling glass houses and an extensive, interactive water system based in part on research into Paxton's gravity-fed water features. The plan diagram (opposite page, lower right) illustrates an interpretation of Paxton's original Geological Time Trail in the park's southeast corner. Primary circulation wends through densely planted hillsides and around lagoon edges with featured views of prehistoric statuary and replicated primeval plantings.

drainage. The terraces' orientation sets up a second major site feature: the original main axis that leads the eye from ordered formality out and down fifty meters to naturalized parkland. In crafting a master plan that responds to the site's theoretical and physical underpinnings, "perception" and "time" became conceptual guides. Perception provides a way to think about, in Neil Porter's words, the "discovery of successive altered images of the spaces and elements within them." The concept of time plays out as active water elements and seasonal plantings that, through their scheduled effects, create a flexible discovery of space that is "a non-constant that spans, stretches, stops, rolls." Due to funding issues the project was restricted to revival of the Geological Time Trail and its dinosaurs in the park's southeast corner.

The process of rehabilitation includes ongoing assessment of lagoon edges, topographic features, pathways, vegetation and dinosaur statuary for optimal integration of historic accuracy and today's

In addition to replanting woodland floors, reconstruction of water edges and paths became much of the project's focus. The firm produced intensively researched documents to guide maintenance of new planting installations. The site's long-term aesthetic vision supports its viability as a place both for interactive natural history education and for urban recreation.

demands. Shorelines are re-graded, reinforced and replanted. The woodland floor is reestablished as a mix of perennial natives and hybrids. Working with plant specialists to track down pre-1850 varieties, an historic rhododendron dell is revived. As one walks the winding, steep stone dust trails that snake around water bodies, climb dramatic knolls, meander through shaded woodland and pass alongside spectral cliffs (all of which double as educational features that offer first-hand experience of historic geological and horticultural materials), it is not difficult to be awed by staged discoveries of nature. It's this sensation – whose creation occupied many of Paxton's contemporaries and persists today as a dominant model for public parks – that Gustafson Porter successfully reintroduces to a portion of the Crystal Palace grounds.

In keeping with tenets of the Picturesque style of Paxton's era, early project statements describe "an exotic ambiance with surprise and discovery" and "a feeling of walking into another time" as critical goals for the Geological Time Trail. Like the 18th-century English landscape gardens, some degree of awareness about the subject matter is needed to fully appreciate what one is looking at: this is one of Gustafson and partners' very few overtly narrative works. At various points along the trail, visitors can view representations of the evolution from early fern varieties that accompanied the dinosaur age to trees and flowering plants of later eras.

Cultuurpark Westergasfabriek, Amsterdam

In the 1960s, the Netherlands discovered vast reserves of natural gas and began to close its coal-gas plants. Westergasfabriek, a 19th-century factory on the outskirts of central Amsterdam, halted operations and in 1981 the site was rezoned as recreation space. The designation was supported by the site's proximity to the city's historic Westerpark and by potential cultural and commercial reuse of its remaining structures (including gas-holding tanks and several outstanding Dutch neo-Renaissance buildings by Isaac Gosschalk). With the long process of functional decontamination underway (a strategy that allows hot spots within a brownfield site to be treated without requiring the costly removal of all soils), a coalition of arts, business and government interests implemented an interim use plan founded upon cultural entrepreneurship. By the mid-1990s, the interim strategy gave way to plans for permanent occupation of buildings and site. Of five design firms invited to envision the open space component of the new culture/recreation park, Kathryn Gustafson

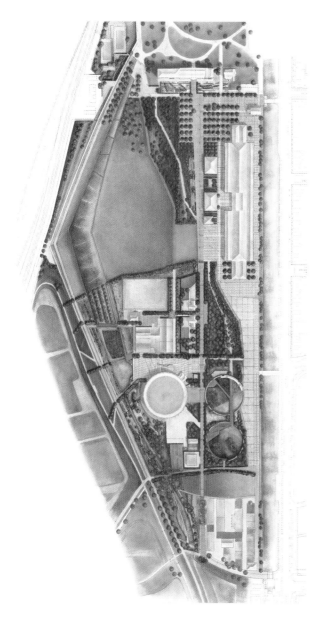

On a roughly trapezoidal site of thirteen hectares, the Cultuurpark Westergasfabriek signals the displacement of industrial operations by new cultural and environmental prerogatives. In the site plan and aerial photo (opposite page), the Stadsdeelraad (town hall) and a portion of the historic Westerpark are seen to the east (at top of images); a grouping of renovated gas plant structures to the south now provide a mixed-use frame for the Market Square, including the purifier building, regulator house, machine and metering buildings; gas holders and the new Cité des Artistes are to the west; raised plots of the Overbracker Polder are seen to the north. Below are views east toward the Stadsdeelraad and across the Haarlemmervaart Canal to the urban beach.

won the commission with "Changement," a proposal produced in collaboration with Francine Houben of Mecanoo architects. In 1997, Gustafson opened an office in London and with partner Neil Porter began to translate concept into detailed design.

"Changement" responded to the park's master plan by offering diverse spatial and temporal experiences. According to the master plan, grounds were to have a green, recreational park function, local residents would be the main users, natural environmental qualities had to be strengthened, and a one-hectare open-air events area must be included. "Changement" was anchored by an axial promenade that transitioned from a formal urban plaza at the east end to an open, naturalized framework that integrated industrial artifacts on the western end adjacent to an existing polder. Written along the bottom of the presentation plan were word progressions that offered a dialog about society's quest for a balanced relationship with

The Events Lake and Wet Gardens comprise a water system that organizes the north side of the park. In contrast to the contained urban form of the Haarlemmervaart canal along the south boundary, the lake expands from a narrow, raised point into a broad, shallow chevron that moves west to the Taxodium Pool, Reed Bed (this page, bottom), Cascade and Stream. Tension between what appears to be straight versus curved edges of water transitions as one changes perspective and perception of the expanse of the water feature. A grass amphitheater embraces the outer edge of the lake, its constructed elevation offers one of the few hills that cyclists encounter along the popular adjacent bike path.

Water is cleansed and then recycled as it passes through the Wet Gardens. Plant species are explicitly framed and punctuated to draw connections between the native palette of the neighboring polder and the hybridized varieties mixed with natives in the gardens. As water appears to transition from the artificial vessel of the lake through progressively naturalized terraces and pools and finally into the winding stream, its movement is engineered in a manner that speaks to the Netherlands' history of water control and land reclamation.

nature. The text read from right to left (from east to west): stad (city), tuin (village), landschap (landscape), natuur (nature) on the first line; politiek (politics), sport/spel (recreation), kunst (art) in the middle; organisatie (order), vrijheid (freedom) on the lowest line.

Using "Changement" as a foundation, Gustafson Porter developed a refined plan that is faithful to the original proposal in its creation of park zones that relate specifically to existing site elements and contexts. At the renovated Stadsdeelraad (town hall), the plaza's layout is a cultivated expression of order. Along the Haarlemmervaart canal, a popular access point for neighborhood residents, a wide, linear urban beach provides public recreation space and connection to the adjacent Market Square. To the southwest, two historic gas-holding structures adjacent to the Cité des Artistes display aquatic plants, fish and reflective water. At the park's northwest corner, proximity to an active agricultural polder generates an explicitly

ecologically oriented circulation scheme and water feature. In its attentiveness to external circum-
stances, the design is a conglomeration of uses – civic, social, commercial, cultural, recreational, ecological –
that operates as a synecdoche for the city rather than the sequential circuit or continuous fabric of a
conventional park.

At the heart of the Westergasfabriek park scheme is the Field of Events. Bounded to the north by the
Events Lake and a grass-sloped amphitheater, the field's scale expands and contracts fluidly as it fills and
empties with people. The Events Lake too fills and empties in response to the park's needs, alternately
reaching up the beached edge or draining to accept crowds. Its figural presence changes as one moves
through the park, offering alternate perceptions of how elements relate to the whole. The south side of the
Field of Events is contained by a mixed woodland through which Broadway moves diagonally in angular

The Reed Garden (opposite page) filters contaminants and carries water toward the western extent of the Wet Gardens, where the aesthetic is reminiscent of the Romantic (below). A series of meticulously detailed, elegantly contemporary bridges and boardwalks designed by Gustafson Porter mark the change from one garden segment to the next. These elements link the adjacent polder and cycle path with walkways and plazas in the Cité des Artistes area of the new park. Overall, the Westergasfabriek scheme meshes the circulation of water and people in a way that references the site's ecological and industrial heritage while providing flexible spaces for both public agenda and individual exploration.

segments. At Market Square, Broadway is interrupted by a swelled land form that introduces a false horizon line to subtly separate spaces and reorient the viewer.

The Westergasfabriek park is closely watched as a model of brownfield reclamation within a physically dense urban context and a programmatically complex set of stakeholders. The scheme has the potential to establish a delicate balance between contamination and accessibility, invention and interpretation, revelation (of the potential of postproductive lands) and renovation (of obsolescence into functionality). As pointed out in the Netherlands Architecture Institute's publication on this project (NAi, 2003), there was no book of instructions. At the time of construction, few precedents existed aside from the IBA Emscher Park and perhaps Bilbao Ria 2000, both operating in quite different contexts and scales. Gustafson Porter's vision of a resilient land is a codependency of engineered nature and industrial artifact.

The Millennium Park design process began in 1997 with a master plan to build subsurface parking and an extension of Edward Bennett's 1922 Beaux-arts Grant Park over existing rail yards, followed by a competition for a progressive garden (one of four contemporary works to be inserted into the park's traditional framework). Located at the parcel's southeast corner, the Lurie Garden documents site history and establishes a new kind of urban environment. The garden within the park brings Chicago's designed public landscapes into the 21st century, joining voices that have contributed to the city's open space agenda such as H. W. S. Cleveland, Frederick Law Olmsted, Daniel Burnham, Jens Jensen and Dan Kiley.

Lurie Garden, Chicago

Hailed as "innovative and site-specific" by Richard Driehaus, sponsor of the Millennium Garden competition, GGN's scheme for the Lurie Garden delves deep into the natural and cultural history of Chicago's shoreline to suggest an optimistic future. The garden is one piece of the 24-acre Millennium Park, a publicly/privately funded reconstruction of the northwest corner of historic Grant Park. In addition to the Lurie Garden, the new park's neo-classical armature holds a massive sculpture by Anish Kapoor, a pair of glass block fountain towers by Jaume Plensa, and a sinuous music pavilion and pedestrian bridge by Frank Gehry. The venerable Art Institute of Chicago (with Renzo Piano's planned north addition) is across Monroe Street. Conceived as a destination landmark, the park sits atop parking structure, occupying the air rights of still-active rail yards below. The scheme presents a third-millennium twist not only on Chicago's historic paradigm of *urbs in horto* but on the legendary physical deformation and reclamation of the city's shoreline. "The site has been

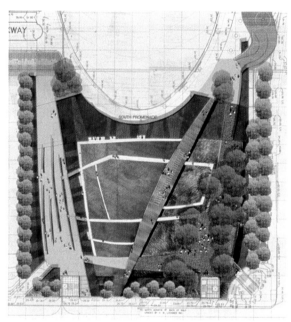

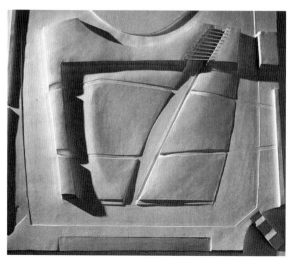

The atmospheric (color, texture, spatial density) and topographical contrasts between the Light Plate (left of center in the plan and model on opposite page) and Dark Plate (right of the diagonal walk) define the inner garden. Visitors move in and through the Dark Plate and its occupied, intimate volume. People move on and over the Light Plate, exposed and able to view out to surrounding areas. The plates operate with the resonance of geomorphology that meets urban intensity; conceptually, what was removed from the lower plate was added to the upper areas. Plantings have up to four feet of soil over structural foam and slab with depths adjusted around perennials and tree pits.

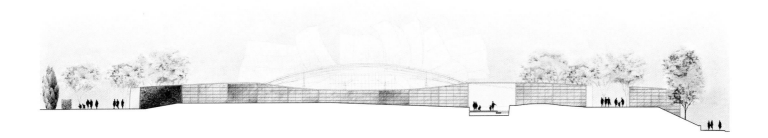

elevated over time," says design partner Shannon Nichol, "from wild, marshy shoreline to railroad yard, to parking garage, to roof garden. The design allows people to experience the contrasts between past and present forms of the site."

The north and west sides of the garden are enclosed by the Shoulder Hedge, a mass of green architecture that rises up to fifteen feet in height and averages sixteen feet in width. The muscular living walls are forcefully although irregularly formal, reading from a distance with the silhouetted coherency of a city skyline. From the Art Institute's windows, the hedge appears as a set of shoulders in relation to the band shell "head" in background. Inside the Shoulder Hedge, the Light Plate elevates to the west, a hopeful rise toward the future. To the east, the Dark Plate paths subside into earth and taller plantings in reference to the shoreline's memory of fluctuating inundation and the historic experience of people's immersion in a landscape volume

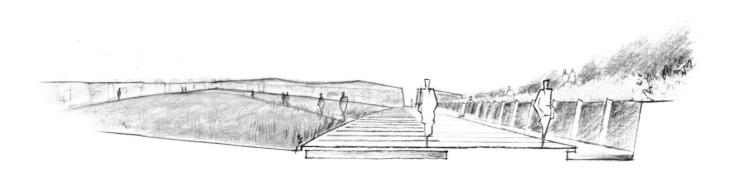

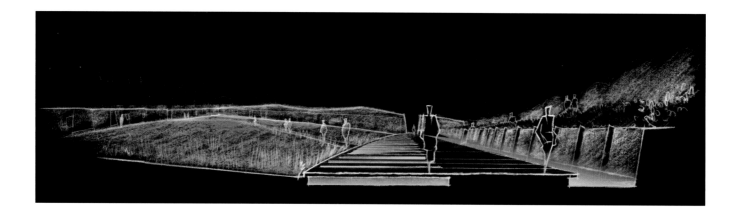

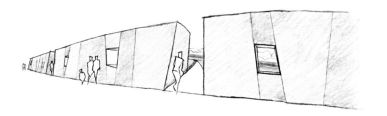

of murky soil and thick vegetation. The Light Plate is a bright, manicured surface planted with horticultural varieties and natives reminiscent of the region's prairies. The plant palette contrasts with the less ordered, denser, leafy spaces of the Dark Plate, while paths flush with the soil level express the use that Chicago now has of the raised landscape. The plates appear to be "punched up" from the ground plane, divided by The Seam and revealing a flesh of solid limestone. In plan view, the linear precision of the shoulder hedge's inside face brings to mind an urban configuration, while in section the garden's ground plane appears as a figure caught post-inhalation, its contours holding deep breaths of site history.

Three primary pedestrian routes link to other areas of Millennium Park, parking and nearby facilities. Extrusion Plaza, along the site's western edge, is inspired by the movement of rail yards and sorts crowds into "packets" or "trains." The Seam boardwalk is suspended over the water channel that divides the two plates

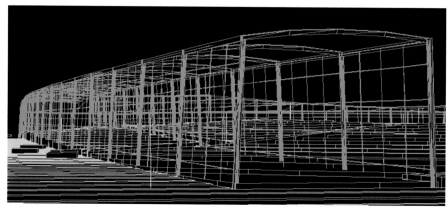

The massive Shoulder Hedge is an artificial horizon line, a protective wall and a back-drop for the inner garden (opposite and below, looking north toward the band shell by Frank Gehry). The hedge is prefigured by a welded steel flat bar clipping guide that will create a slightly battered, continuous asymmetry over time (opposite page, bottom). The hedge's mixed evergreen and deciduous varieties will take ten to twenty years to fully mature. Seating alcoves modulate the green walls (opposite, top). Seasonal plantings and lighting effects conceived jointly by GGN, Piet Oudolf, Robert Israel and other consultants intensify features of the garden, enabling it as an urban landmark that is active year-round, day and night.

across the site's heart. The Cloud Plaza occupies the site's eastern side. Secondary pathways give access to areas removed from the main thoroughfares. To a greater degree than early Gustafson projects and used with increasing frequency as a GGN design strategy, at the Lurie Garden plants are simultaneously formal devices that create space and a narrative medium that relays information about a site's context, history and conceptual framework. The experience of the user is prioritized, welcoming a visitor to take in the movement of contour lines, the shape of the earth and the tactile qualities of water, stone and plants. Here perception *becomes* thematic narrative, a condition achieved in large part through the contributions of master plantsman Piet Oudolf and theater set maestro Robert Israel. Living land form, botanical lyricism and dramatic illumination give the Lurie Garden its voice year-round and across the hours of the day.

In gaining the project commission, Gustafson Porter became responsible for the design of an area that is 22,000 square meters/5.4 acres. The project boundaries include the garden itself (14,000 square meters/3.5 acres) as well as the redesign of surrounding streets. An important aspect of the scheme's initial concept is the idea of Lebanon's journey from a fragile puzzle shattered by war to a country gaining unity and peace under the will of its people (opposite page). Cultural exchange, both friendly and forced, has defined Lebanon's history, and to the design team Beirut is a microcosm of the nation's political, social and physical landscape. The garden is an opportunity to bring diverse people and cultural fragments together to heal.

Hadiqat As-Samah, Beirut

At the close of the 20th century, Beirut was a fractured city intent on healing, in part through the construction of new public spaces. In 1999, Gustafson Porter joined a limited competition for a public garden and visitor center in the heart of the central district. The site, as Kathryn Gustafson and Neil Porter discovered on their first visit, was intensely layered with remnants of past civilizations. While other firms proposed to float above or frame the ancient ruins, Gustafson Porter collaborated with an archeologist and won the commission with a scheme that directly interacts with history. In Neil Porter's words, the project requires "both the emotional involvement of the insider and the detachment of the outsider."

The process began with site excavation at a depth of up to five meters. Each layer removed revealed different (hi)stories: first the medieval city walls along the eastern boundary of the site, next a Roman street grid, and finally, Hellenistic retaining walls whose curved lines hugged bedrock contours. The modern-day

context includes three mosques, three cathedrals, and the Nourieh Shrine (a shrine to Mary used by both Christian and Muslim women) that overlook the sunken site. After exploratory excavation, delicate zones in the southwest quadrant were protected while other areas to the north were reburied to preserve their archeology and to make ground for the new gardens. The multi-tiered site presents pieces of the past, present and future that for the people of Beirut can be a rediscovery of deep culture and real hope.

Beyond the dialog of past and future, the physiography of Lebanon plays an important role in the scheme's spatial organization in plan and section. How can one find forgiveness for the person who fought against them or hurt their family in the past? Inspired in part by project founder Alexandra Asseily's idea that forgiveness is a liberating act that gives humans the capacity for peace, the designer team chose to step outside contentious religious issues to search for common ground. The common ground they found

Remains are exposed in the lower, southern half of the garden (existing conditions in foreground below), with localized fill for new paths and planting. New structures such as a pergola and walkways are inserted within to accentuate the layered remains (opposite page). With new protective surfacing spectacular remnants of the Cardo Maximus (running north-south) and the secondary Decumanus (running east-west) are used as primary circulation for the archeological garden. Remains of Roman *domus* and workshops on either side of the Decumanus become small discovery gardens. Hellenistic sandstone blocks frame an ancient well that floods in winter creating a seasonal terrace that measures water levels.

is people's love, pride and belief in their land. Using this as a starting point – Lebanon's snow-capped mountains descend into cultivated lands and dense settlement along the rocky Mediterranean coast – the nation's terrain and vegetation was translated into a sequence of experiences within the garden.

At the garden's highest point, the north entry opens into a walled garden that is an initiation or threshold. One must pass between walls and over water before reaching the rest of the garden. Walkways frame a broad pool, bringing visitors through a wet, humid zone before the main axis ramps down into successive terraced plantations of native trees from the mountain region, a rich variety of olive and fruit groves, and citrus trees from the coastal plains. The garden's atmosphere becomes increasingly arid as one moves from the walled north garden down through the terraces, to Hadiqat As-Samah Square and into the south archeological garden. The overlay of two conceptual approaches – the vernacular of a regional landscape

At the site's narrow waist (site plan, page 190), a pre-existing pedestrian thoroughfare passes above Hadiqat As-Samah Square, the forecourt to the Visitor Center tucked below the west promenade.

Bordered by a perfect square of water fed by irrigation rills? from above, the plaza's paved surface is inscribed with outlines of underlying ruins. At the site's north entrance, a shallow pool with water jets

and a lotus garden greets visitors. Its cruciform walkways are reminiscent of early paradise gardens (specifically recalling Fahkradine, a 17th-century water garden that once

occupied the site). An amphitheater, access ramps, and restaurant terraces engage the garden from the multi-tiered perimeter at its southern half (opposite page).

(materiality of place) and an engagement between present and past (a dialog of time) – resonates with words from Kahlil Gibran's *The Prophet* that were featured in Gustafson Porter's competition entry: "Let us today embrace the past with remembrance and the future with longing."

The garden is designed both for visual and experiential discovery. Ramped access at both ends of the garden prevents a singular, prioritized view, while on the east and west sides the design scheme uses dramatic sectional differentials as opportunities to create plays of light and vegetal texture. The Hadiqat As-Samah/Garden of Forgiveness exists because of devastation, excavation, interpretation and translation. Its presence in the heart of Beirut is a reminder of the tension between destruction and creation, processes which, as Octavio Paz says, are synonymous in the eyes of the gods.

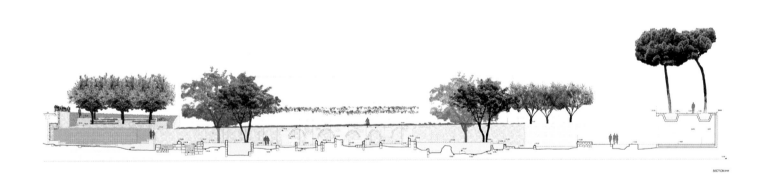

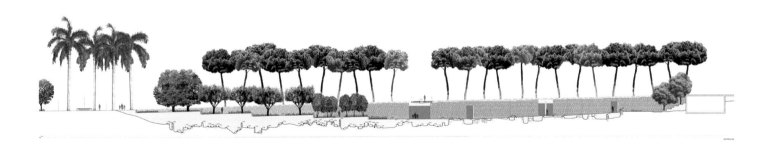

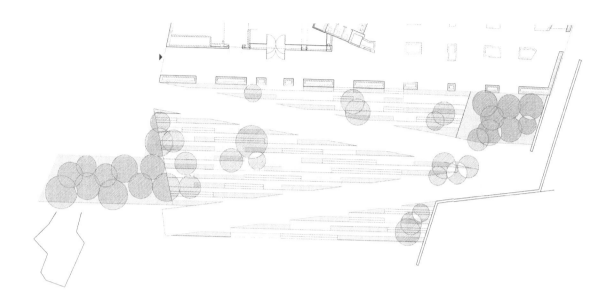

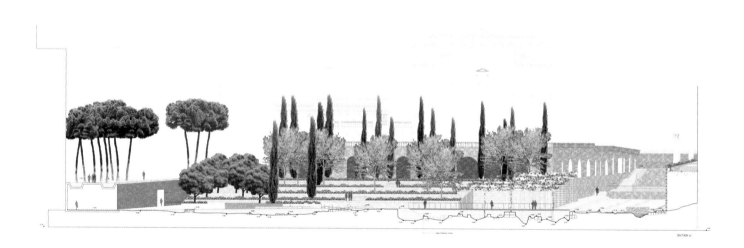

List of Projects

The list is arranged alphabetically, according to the project name abbreviations assigned by the offices.

Art Institute of Chicago, New North Wing Courtyard and Streetscape AIC
Date estimated completion: 2007
Project name: Art Institute of Chicago New North Wing Addition
Project location: Chicago, IL, USA
Client: Art Institute of Chicago
Size: 13,200 sf / 1,226 m²
Project Team:
   GGN: Managing Partner/Design Partner: Jennifer Guthrie
   Reviewing Design Partners: Shannon Nichol, Kathryn Gustafson
   Project Team: Gareth Loveridge, Ian Horton, Yi-Chun Lin Stanley
Building Architects: Renzo Piano Building Workshop
Architect of Record: Interactive Design
Structural Engineer: Arup

Court of Appeals Courtyard, Aix-en-Provence AIX
Date completed: 1995
Project name: Cour d'Appel
Project location: Aix-en-Provence, France
Client: Cour d'Appel d'Aix-en-Provence
Size: 400 m² / 4,306 sf
Project Team:
   Lead Design: Kathryn Gustafson
   Project Landscape Architect: Philippe Marchand Isabelle Lafuma
Architect: Jean Michel Battesti Architectes et Associés
Architect: Roubert - Dumont - Blehaut Architectes Associés

Arthur Ross Terrace at the American Museum of Natural History, New York AMN
Date completed: 2000
Project name: Arthur Ross Terrace
Project location: New York, NY, USA
Client: American Museum of Natural History
Size: 47,114 sf / 4,380 m²
Architect Representative:
Architects for the Rose Center for Earth and Space: Polshek Partnership Architects
Lead Design: Kathryn Gustafson
Project Team:
   Landscape Architect of Record:
   Anderson & Ray, Inc
   Principal In-Charge: Charles Anderson
   Project Team: Christopher Overdorf, Shannon Nichol, Kevin Pfeiffer
Contractor Representative: Morse Diesel International, Inc. (now AMEC)
Structural: Weidlinger Associates, Inc.
Lighting: Fisher Marantz Stone
Fountain Designer: Gerald Palevsky

"Breast Plate", Tunnel Entrance, near Paris BPL
Date of design: 1993 – unbuilt
Project name: Breast Plate
Location: A86 corridor between Rueil-Malmaison + A13 highway, France
Client: Cofiroute France
Size: 15 acres / 6 ha
Project Team:
   Lead Design: Kathryn Gustafson
   Project Manager: Sylvie Farges
   Melissa Brown Lacoast
   Illustrations and Perspectives: Franck Neau

Seattle Civic Center CHS
Date estimated completion: Phase one: 2003
Phase two: 2004
Phase three: TBD
Project name: Seattle Civic Center
Project location: Seattle, WA, USA
Client: City of Seattle
Size: 278,000 sf / 6.4 acres / 25,800 m²
Project Team:
   GGN: Managing Partner: Jennifer Guthrie
   Reviewing Design Partner: Shannon Nichol
   Senior Design Partner: Kathryn Gustafson
   Senior Project Manager: Marcia West
   Project Team: Gareth Loveridge, Alan McWain, Rodrigo Abela, Anita Madtes, Erik Hanson
Consulting Landscape Architect: Swift & Company Landscape Architects
Architect: City Hall: Bohlin Cywinski Jackson
Architect of Record: City Hall: Bassetti Architects
Architect: Justice Center: NBBJ
General Contractor: Hoffman Construction Co.
Civil Engineer: SVR Design Co.
Structural Glass Engineers: Dewhurst Macfarlane and Partners, Inc.
Structural Engineer: KPFF Consulting Engineers
Mechanical Engineer: Wood/Harbinger, Inc.
Electrical Engineer: Sparling
Fountain Designer: CMS Collaborative
Lighting Designer: Fisher Marantz Stone
Specification Writer: Eskilsson Architecture
Cost Estimator: Davis Langdon Adamson
Acoustical Engineer: The Greenbusch Group
Lead Artist, Justice Center: Pam Beyette
Lead Artist, City Hall: Beliz Brother

Justice Center Seattle (part of Seattle Civic Center)
Date completed: 2003
Project name: Seattle Justice Center Plaza
Project location: Seattle, WA, USA
Client: City of Seattle
Size: 31,975 sf / 2,970 m²
Project Team:
   GGN: Managing Partner: Jennifer Guthrie
   Reviewing Design Partner: Shannon Nichol
   Senior Design Partner: Kathryn Gustafson
   Senior Project Manager: Marcia West

Project Team: Gareth Loveridge, Alan McWain, Rodrigo Abela, Anita Madtes
Consulting Landscape Architect:
Swift & Company Landscape Architects
Architect: NBBJ
General Contractor: Hoffman Construction Co.
Civil Engineer: SVR Design Co.
Structural Glass Engineer: Dewhurst Macfarlane and Partners, Inc.
Structural Engineer: KPFF Consulting Engineers
Mechanical Engineer: Wood/Harbinger, Inc.
Electrical Engineer: Sparling
Fountain Designer: CMS Collaborative
Lighting Designer: Fisher Marantz Stone
Specification Writer: Eskilsson Architecture
Cost Estimator: Davis Langdon Adamson
Acoustical Engineer: The Greenbusch Group
Lead Artist: Pam Beyette

Seattle City Hall (part of Seattle Civic Center)
Date estimated completion: 2004
Project name: Seattle City Hall
Project location Seattle, WA, USA
Client: City of Seattle
Size: 31,000 sf / 2,880 m²
Project Team:
   GGN: Managing Partner: Jennifer Guthrie
   Reviewing Design Partner: Shannon Nichol
   Senior Design Partner: Kathryn Gustafson
   Senior Project Manager: Marcia West
   Project Team: Gareth Loveridge, Alan McWain, Rodrigo Abela, Erik Hanson
Consulting Landscape Architect: Swift & Company Landscape Architects
Lead Architect: Peter Bohlin, Bohlin Cywinski Jackson
Architect of Record: Bassetti Architects
General Contractor: Hoffman Construction Co.
Civil Engineer: SVR Design Co.
Structural Glass Engineer: Dewhurst Macfarlane and Partners, Inc.
Structural Engineer: KPFF Consulting Engineers
Mechanical Engineer: Wood/Harbinger, Inc.
Electrical Engineer: Sparling
Fountain Consultant: CMS Collaborative
Lighting Designer: Sparling, Fisher Marantz Stone
Specification Writer: Eskilsson Architecture
Cost Estimator: Davis Langdon Adamson
Acoustical Engineer: The Greenbusch Group
Metal Fabricator/Installer: George Third & Son
Lead Artist: Beliz Brother
Stone Supplier/Installer: Columbia Stone Incorporated

Crystal Palace Park, London CRY
Date completed: 2002
Project name: Crystal Palace Park
Project location: London, UK
Client: Robbie Stoakes, Director of Community and
Leisure Services, London Borough of Bromley
Size: 42, 000 m² / 10.4 acres
Project Team:
   Gustafson Porter: Kathryn Gustafson/Neil Porter,
   Frances Christie, Peter Culley, Philippe Marchand,
   Charlotte Martin, Rachel Mooney
Architect: John Lyall Architects
Project Management: Alan Baxter and Associates
Cost Consultant: Northcroft
Structural and Mechanical Engineer:
Alan Baxter and Associates
Soil Scientist: Soil and Land Consultants

Electricité de France (EDF) Pylons, France EDF
Date completed: 2002
1998: prototype completed
1992: competition
Project name: Electricité de France (EDF) –
high-tension pylon
Project location: France
Client: EDF – Electricité de France
Project Team:
   Lead Design: Kathryn Gustafson,
   Ian Ritchie, Henry Bardsley
   Design Team: Mitsu Edwards, Emmanuelle Floch,
   Dan Burr, Cécile Boudan
Architect: Ian Ritchie Architects
Consulting Engineer: RFR

Esso Headquarters Garden, Rueil-Malmaison ESS
Date completed: 1992
Project name: Esso Headquarters
Project location: Rueil-Malmaison, France
Client: Esso S.A.F. / Mobil Oil Française
Size: 2.7 acres / 118,407 sf / 1.1 ha
Lead Design: Kathryn Gustafson
Project Team:
   Landscape Architects: C. Barthelmebs, Gérard Pras
   Project Manager: Sylvie Farges
Architect: Viguier Jodry et Associés

Square Rachimaninov, Quartier de L'Evangile, Paris
EVA
Date completed: 1991
Project name: L'Evangile (renamed Square
Rachmaninov)
Project location: Paris, 18th arrondissement, France
Client: Ville de Paris
Size: 0.7 ha / 1.7 acres
Project Team:
   Design Lead: Kathryn Gustafson
   Project Manager: Sylvie Farges
Landscape Architect: Charles Gardner

Rights of Man Square, Evry EVR
Date completed: 1991
Project name: Place des Droits de l'Homme, Evry
Client: Ville d'Evry
Project location: Place des Droits de l'Homme
et du Citoyen, Evry, France
Size: 3 acres / 129,170 sf / 1.2 ha
Project Team:
   Lead Design: Kathryn Gustafson
   Project Architect: Gérard Pras
   Project manager: Sylvie Farges
   Design Team: C. Bartelmebs
   Karl Brugmann, Violaine Liétard
Engineer: Setec (Société d'Etudes Techniques
et Economiques)

Hadiqat As-Samah, Beirut GFB
Date estimated completion: 2005
Project name: Garden of Forgiveness
Project location: Beirut, Lebanon
Client: Solidere Size:
6.2 acres / 21,500 m² / 270,000 sf / 2.5 ha
Project Team:
   Gustafson Porter: Kathryn Gustafson/Neil Porter,
   Neil Black, Frances Christie, Paula Craft,
   Nick Hughes, Max Norman, Nilesh Patel,
   Jose Rosa, Julia Wessendorf
Concept Design Engineer: Arup
Construction Engineer: Dar Al-Handasah Engineers
Archaeology Consultancy: Arup / Historic Lebanon
Archaeology and Architectural Coordination:
YAA (Yaser Abun-Nasr)

L'Oréal Garden, Aulnay-sous-Bois LOR
Date completed: 1992
Project name: Usine de la Barbière
Project location: Aulnay-sous-Bois, France
Client: L'Oréal
Size: 3.7 acres / 161,460 sf / 1.5 ha
Project Team:
   Lead Design: Kathryn Gustafson
   Project Landscape Architect: Isabelle Lafuma
   Project Manager: Sylvie Farges, Violaine Liétard
Building Architect: Valode & Pistre Architectes
Engineer: Arup

"Landing Pad for Ideas", Paris LPI
Date of competition: June 1988, Ideas competition
for the French Revolution Bicentennial; project
selected for Inventer 89 exhibition by the French
government – unbuilt
Project name: Aire d'atterrissage des idées
Location: Paris, 12th arrondissement, France
Project Team:
   Kathryn Gustafson & Charles Gardner

Les Pennes: City Entrance to Marseille MAR
Date completed: 2003
Project name: Les Pennes-Mirabeau
Project location: Freeway interchange of A7 and
A55, north of Marseille, France
Current owner: Direction Département de
l'Equipement – DDE Bouches-du-Rhône
Client: DDE Bouches-du-Rhône
Size: 30 ha / 75 acres
Project Team:
   Lead Design: Kathryn Gustafson
   Architects: Pierre Solbes, Philippe Marchand
   Project Manager: Sylvie Farges
   Renderings: Melissa Brown
CAD Advisor: Spencer Hunt

Lurie Garden, Chicago MGC
Date completed: 2004
Project name: Lurie Garden
Project location: Millennium Park, Chicago, IL, USA
Client: Millennium Park, Inc.
Project Director: Mr. Edward Uhlir, FAIA
Donor: The Ann and Robert H. Lurie Family
Foundation
Size: 3 acres / 135,940 sf / 1.2 ha
Construction Management: Spectrum Strategies:
Chicago, IL
Project Team:
   GGN: Senior Design Partner: Kathryn Gustafson
   Design Partner: Shannon Nichol
   Managing Partner: Jennifer Guthrie
   Project Team: Gareth Loveridge, David Nelson,
   Rodrigo Abela
Perennial Planting Design: Piet Oudolf
Conceptual Review: Robert Israel
(Theater Set Designer)
Contractor: Walsh Construction
Structural and Civil Engineer: KPFF Consulting
Engineers
Mechanical and Electrical Engineer: EME, LLC
Fountain Designer: CMS Collaborative
Lighting Designer: Schuler & Shook, Inc.
Specification Writer: ArchiTech
Cost Estimator: Davis Langdon Adamson
Irrigation Designer: Jeffrey L. Bruce & Company
Local Landscape Architect: Terry Guen Design
Associates

**Kreielsheimer Promenade and South Terrace
at Marion Oliver McCaw Hall, Seattle** MOM
Date completion: 2003
Project name: Kreielsheimer Promenade and
South Terrace
Project location: Seattle, WA, USA
Client: Seattle Center Foundation
Size: 45,000 sf / 4,037 m² / 0.4 ha / 1 acre
Project Team:
   GGN: Design Partner: Kathryn Gustafson
   Collaborating Design Partner: Shannon Nichol

22

Senior Project Manager: Marcia West
Project Team: Gareth Loveridge
Building Architect: LMN Architects
Civil Engineer: AKB Engineers
Structural Engineer: Skilling
Mechanical Engineer: CDi
Electrical Engineer: Sparling
Water Feature Engineer: Brown & Caldwell
Lighting: Leni Schwendinger, Light Projects Ltd
Cost Estimator: Rider Hunt Levett & Bailey
General Contractor: Baugh / Skanska USA

Retention Basin and Park, Morbras MOR
Date completed: 1986
Project name: Morbras – Meeting Point
Project location: Pontault-Combault and
Roissy-en-Brie, Seine-et-Marne, France
Client: DDE Seine-et-Marne
Size: 35 ha / 86.5 acres
Lead Design: Kathryn Gustafson
Landscape Team: Bertrand Paulet
Project Manager: Sylvie Farges
Technical Model Consultant: Sean Dunbar

**Great Glass House Interior, National Botanic
Garden of Wales** NBW
Date completed: 1999
Project name: Great Glass House (interior),
National Botanic Garden of Wales
Project location: Llanarthne, Carmarthenshire,
Wales, UK
Client: Charles Stirton, Director, National Botanic
Garden of Wales
Size: 37,700 sf / 3,500 m²
Project Team:
  Interior Landscape Consultant: Gustafson Porter:
  Kathryn Gustafson, Peter Culley, Rachel Mooney,
  Neil Porter
Building Architect: Foster and Partners
Structural Engineer: Anthony Hunt Associates
Mechanical Engineer: Max Fordham and Partners
Project Manager: Schal International Management
Horticultural Consultants: Charles Stirton, Ivor
Stokes

North End Parks, Boston NEP
Date estimated completion: 2006
Project name: North End Parks
Project location: Boston, MA, USA
Client: Massachusetts Turnpike Authority
Size: 122,053 sf / 11,339 m² 2.8 acres / 1.13 ha
Project Team:
  GGN: Design Partner: Shannon Nichol
  Reviewing Design Partner: Kathryn Gustafson
  Senior Project Manager: Marcia West
  Project Team: Emily Pizzuto, Mischa Ickstadt,
  Erik Hanson, Rodrigo Abela
Landscape Architect of Record: Crosby Schlessinger

& Smallridge, LLC
Structural Engineer: Earth Tech
Mechanical, Civil and Electrical Engineer:
DMC Engineering, Inc.
Fountain Design: Atlantic Fountains
Fountain Consultant: CMS Collaborative
Lighting Designer: Ripman Lighting Consultants
Historic Interpretation: American History Workshop
Graphic Design: Selbert Perkins Design

Passy PAS
Date completed: Not built
Project name: Passy
Project Location: Paris, 16th arrondissement, France
Client: Fougerolles, Private Developer
General Contractor: N/A
Size: 3.7 acres / 1.5 ha
Project Team:
  Lead Design: Kathryn Gustafson
  Project Landscape Architect: Philippe Marchand
  Project Manager: Sylvie Farges
Architect: Francis Soler & Bertrand Bonnier

**Diana, Princess of Wales Memorial Fountain,
London** PDM
Date completed: 2004
Project name: Diana, Princess of Wales
Memorial Fountain
Project location: Hyde Park, London, UK
Client: Department of Culture, Media & Sport,
Royal Parks
Project Sponsor: The Royal Parks
Size: 60,278 sf / 5,600 m² / .5 ha / 1.3 acres
Project Team:
  Gustafson Porter: Kathryn Gustafson/Neil Porter,
  Mary Bowman, Frances Christie,
  Mark Gillingham, Tamara Hall, Max Norman,
  Jose Rosa, Julia Wessendorf
Engineer: Arup: Ian Carradice, Nick Jeffries,
David Short, Borbala Trifunovics
Project Manager: Bucknall Austin Project
Management
Main Contractor: Geoffrey Osborne Ltd.
Fountain Subcontractor: Ocmis
Landscape Contractor: Willerby Landscapes
Stone Layers: Cathedral Works Organisation
Stone Masons: S McConnell and Sons
Stone Texturing Specialists: Barron Gould – Texxus
Surface Modelling: Surface Development
Engineering Ltd.
Soil Scientist: Soil and Land Consultants
Hydraulic Modelling: Professor David Hardwick
Collaborating Artist: Shelagh Wakely

Swiss Cottage Open Space, London SCG
Date estimated completion: 2005
Project name: Swiss Cottage Open Space
Project location: Avenue Road, London NW3, UK
Client: Ian McNicol

Director of Leisure and Community Services,
London Borough of Camden
Size: 1 ha, one of four Gustafson Porter designed
linked projects which form part of the Swiss Cottage
Development
Project Team:
  Gustafson Porter: Kathryn Gustafson/Neil Porter,
  Mary Bowman, Neil Black, Frances Christie,
  Sibylla Hartel, Stephaan Lambreghts, Kinna
  Stallard, John Smart
Project Manager: J W Project Services
Civil and Structural Engineers: whitbybird
Mechanical and Electrical Engineers:
Gifford and Partners
Cost Consultant: EC Harris
Fountain Subcontractor: Invent Water Treatment Ltd
Collaborating Artist: Martin Richman

Private Garden PR
Date completed: 2004
Project name: Private Residence
Client & Project location: Confidential
Size: 38,200 sf / 3,550 m²
Project Team:
  GGN: Design Partner: Shannon Nichol
  Reviewing Design Partner: Kathryn Gustafson
  Senior Project Manager: Marcia West
  Project Team: Alan McWain
Architect: Olson Sundberg Kundig Allen Architects
General Contractor: An Urban Company
Landscape Contractor: Planting Design
Civil Engineer: Robert Foley and Associates
Structural Engineer: Monte Clarke Engineering
Mechanical Engineer: Keen Engineering
Electrical Engineer: Paragon & Mogul Electric
Company
Geotechnical Consultant: Associated Earth Sciences
Surveyor: Geodimensions, Inc.
Lighting Design: Studio Lux

**South Coast Plaza Bridge and Strata Garden,
Costa Mesa** SCP
Date completed: 2000
Project name: South Coast Plaza Garden Terrace
and Pedestrian Bridge
Project location: Costa Mesa, CA, USA
Client: C. J. Segerstrom & Sons
Size: Plaza: 26,000 sf / 2415 m² Bridge: 560 lf / 170 ml
Lead Design: Kathryn Gustafson
Project Collaborators:
  Landscape Architect of Record: Anderson and Ray
  Principal in Charge: Stephen Ray
  Designer: Jennifer Guthrie
  Project Team: Inge Kaufmann, Shaney Clemmons,
  Shannon Nichol, Christopher Overdorf
Architect: Ellerbe Becket: James Poulson
Contractor Representative: Bayley Construction
Bridge Engineer: HNTB Corporation
Civil Engineer: RBF

Structural Engineer: Robert Englekirk
Mechanical Engineer: Tsuchiyama & Kaino
Electrical Engineer: FBA Engineering
Fountain Designer: CMS Collaborative
Lighting Designer: Francis Krahe & Associates
Specification Consultant: Brown and Sanchis

"Wind, Sound and Movement" – SF MoMA SFM
Date completed: Temporary exhibition:
May – October, 2001
Project name: "Wind, Sound and Movement"
– San Francisco Museum of Modern Art "Revelatory
Landscapes" Exhibition
Curators: Aaron Betsky, Leah Levy
Location: Harney Way & Jamestown Avenue,
San Francisco, CA, USA
Client: San Francisco Museum of Modern Art
Size: N/A
Project Team:
    Design: Kathryn Gustafson, Jaimi Baer
    Project Team: Rodrigo Abela, Kevin Conger &
    Will Moss, Jeanne Ernst
Consulting Landscape Architect: Conger Moss
Guillard Landscape Architects
Architect: Jaimi Baer
General Contractor: Dawn Landscaping Inc.

Shell Headquarters Garden, Rueil-Malmaison SHE
Date completed: 1991
Project name: Shell Petroleum Headquarters
Current Owner: Schneider Electric + IFP
Project location: Rueil-Malmaison, France
Client: Shell Petroleum
Size: 6.2 acres / 2.5 ha
Lead Design: Kathryn Gustafson
    Project Team: Sylvie Farges, Melissa Brown
    Lacoast, Karl Brugmann
Architect: Valode & Pistre Architectes

Thames Barrier Park, London TBP
Date of competition: 1995 – unbuilt
Project name: Thames Barrier Park
Client: LDC London Docklands Corporation
Location: Docklands, London, UK
Size: 13 ha / 32 acres
Project Team:
    Kathryn Gustafson
    Project Architect: Philippe Marchand, Anton James
    Presentation Illustrations: Franck Neau
Collaborating Artist: Jane Kelly

Courtyards, Government offices Great George
Street, London TCL
Date completed: 2004
Project name: GOGGS Courtyards.
Project location: Westminster, London, UK
Client: Exchequer Partnership plc

Size: Approximately 960 m² / 10,333 sf per courtyard
Project Team:
    Gustafson Porter: Neil Porter,
    Kathryn Gustafson, Mary Bowman, David Buck,
    Tamara Hall, Sibylla Hartel, Mieke Tanghe
Architect: Foster and Partners
Project Management: Bovis Lend Lease
Cost Consultant: Atkins Faithful and Gould
Structural Engineer: Waterman Partnership
Mechanical Engineer: Waterman Gore
Main Contractor: Bovis Lend Lease
Fountain Subcontractor: Ocmis
Lighting Consultant: Spiers and Majors

Seattle Theater District TD
Date completed: Master plan, 2002
Project name: Theater District Plan
Project location: Seattle Center, Seattle, WA, USA
Client: Seattle Center Foundation
Size: 8 city blocks, 2 ha / 4.8 acres
Project Team:
    GGN: Senior Design Partner: Kathryn Gustafson
    Design Partner: Shannon Nichol
    Project Team: Gareth Loveridge
Architect: Weinstein Copeland Architects
Collaborating Landscape Architects:
The Berger Partnership
Lighting Designer: Ross De Alessi Lighting Design
Project Management: Jerry Ernst Associates

Gardens of the Imagination, Terrasson TER
Date completed: 1995
Project name: Les Jardins de l'Imaginaire
Project location: Terrasson, Dordogne, France
Client: Ville de Terrasson – Lavilledieu
Size: 14.8 acres / 6 ha
Lead Design: Kathryn Gustafson
Project Team:
    Project Landscape Architect: Philippe Marchand
    Project Manager: Sylvie Farges
    Project Team: Emmanuelle Floch, Anton James,
    Isabelle Lafuma, Franck Neau
Architect, Exhibition Building: Ian Ritchie
Collaborating Sculptor: Peter Forakis

Parc de la Villette, Cité des Sciences et de
l'Industrie Greenhouse, Paris VIS
Date completed: 1986
Project name: Parc de la Villette – serre
Project location: Parc de la Villette – Glasshouse on
South Façade of the Museum of Science and
Industry, Paris, France
Client: Etablissement Public du Parc de la Villette
Size: 1,920 m² / 20,666 sf
Project Team:
    Design: Kathryn Gustafson, Ian Ritchie
    Project Manager: Sylvie Farges
    Project Architect: Karl Brugmann

Consulting Engineers: RFR; Peter Rice, Henry
Bardsley, Guillermo Wieland

Cultuurpark Westergasfabriek, Amsterdam WPA
Date completed: 2004
Project name: Westergasfabriek Park
Project location: Haarlemmerweg, Amsterdam,
The Netherlands
Client: Evert Verhagen, Projectbureau
Westergasfabriek, Westerpark District Council
& City of Amsterdam
Size: 11.5 ha / 28 acres
Project Team:
    Gustafson Porter: Kathryn Gustafson/Neil Porter,
    Neil Black, Juanita Cheung, Frances Christie,
    Philippe Marchand, Gerben Mienis,
    Rachel Mooney, Mieke Tanghe, Pauline Wieringa
Architect: Francine Houben, Mecanoo
Concept Design Engineer: Arup
Structural Engineer: Pieters Bouwtechniek
Construction Engineer: Tauw (Rene Vilijn)
Design Project Management: Northcroft Belgium sa
Construction Project Management: Tauw (Rene Vilijn)
General contractor: Marcus bv
Translator: Claudia Ruitenberg
Specification Writer: Bugel Hajima

Wind and Sound Garden, Lausanne WSG
Date: Temporary Installation: March – October 1997
Project name: Wind and Sound Garden for the first
Festival du Jardin Urbain
Location: Lausanne, Switzerland
Project Team:
    Lead Design: Kathryn Gustafson
    Architect: Philippe Marchand
    Sound: François Paris, composer

People

Rodrigo Abela
CHS, NEP, SFM, MGC

Yaser Abun-Nasr
GFB

Audrey Adeyemi
GP office

Jane Amidon
Author of *Moving
Horizons*

Virginia Anderson
MOM, TD

Charles Anderson
AMN, SCP

Alexandra Asseily
GFB

Jaimi Baer
SFM

Lesley Bain
TD

Sarah Bannock
GP office

Henry Bardsley
EDF, VIS

Linda Barron
PDM

Caroline Barthelmebs
ESS, EVR

Aaron Betsky
SFM, Essay – *Moving
Horizons*

Pam Beyette
CHS

Richard Bickers
WPA

Neil Black
WPA, GFB, SCG

Peter Bohlin
CHS

Cécile Boudan
EDF

Mary Bowman
PDM, SCG,TCL

Marilyn Brockman
CHS

Beliz Brother
CHS

Melissa Brown Lacoast
BPL, SHE

Karl Brugmann
EVR, SHE, VIS

John Bryan
AIC, MGC

David Buck
CRY, TCL

Dominik Bueckers
MN

Janet Burley
GP office

Dan Burr
EDF

Ian Carradice
PDM

Bill Caskey
SCP

Frances Christie
CRY, WPA, GFB,
PDM, SCG

Juanita Cheung
WPA

Shaney Clemmons
SCP

Kevin Conger
SFM

Paula Craft GFB	Tyler Donaldson AMN	Jerry Ernst TD	Emmanuelle Floch EDF, TER, WSG	Angus Gavin GFB	Tamara Hall TCL, PDM	Nick Hughes GFB
Deneen Crosby NEP	Jan Drago CHS	Michael Espenan GGN office	Norman Foster TCL, NBW	Mark Gillingham PDM	Erik Hanson CHS, NEP	Spencer Hunt MAR
Peter Culley CRY, NBW	Sean Dunbar MOR	Sylvie Farges BPL, ESS, EVA, EVR, LOR, MAR, MOR, SHE, TER, VIS, PAS	Peter Forakis TER	John Gould PDM	Sibylla Hartel SCG, TCL	Mischa Ickstadt NEP
Margot d'Aboville GP	Mitsu Edwards EDF		Charles Gardner EVA, LPI	Kathryn Gustafson	Ian Horton AIC	Robert Israel MGC
Spencer de Grey TCL, NBW	Jeanne Ernst SFM, MN	Bob Fernandez SCP	Steve Gaukroger WPA	Jennifer Guthrie AIC, CHS, MGC, SCP	Francine Houben WPA	Anton James TBP, TER
		Joseph Fleischer AMN				

Ali Jeevanjee
SCP

Nick Jeffries
PDM

Ken Johnsen
CHS

Michael Jones
NBW

Robert Jones
AIC

Oussama Kabbani
GFB

Nieven Kadry
GP office

Inge Kaufmann
SCP

Jane Kelly
TBP

Isabelle Lafuma
AIX, LOR, TER

Monica Lake
CHS

Stephaan Lambreghts
SCG

Leah Levy
SFM, author of
Sculpting the Land

Violaine Liétard
EVR, LOR

Yi-Chun Lin Stanley
GGN, AIC

Tina Lindinger
CHS

Emma Lipscombe
GP

Gareth Loveridge
AIC, CHS, MGC,
MOM, TD

John Lowery
AMN

John Lyall
CRY

Tim Macfarlane
CHS

Anita Madtes
CHS

Philippe Marchand
AIX, CAR, CRY, MAR,
TBP, TER, WPA,
WSG, PAS

Charlotte Martin
CRY

Alan McWain
CHS, PR

Gerben Mienis
WPA

Rachel Mooney
CRY, NBW, WPA

Andreas Müller
Editor of *Moving
Horizons*

Franck Neau
BPL, TER

David Nelson
MCG

Shannon Nichol
AIC, AMN, CHS, MGC,
MOM, NEP, PR, TD, SCP

Max Norman
GFB, PDM

Tim O'Hare
CRY, WPA, PMD

Lynda Olson
GGN office

Jim Olson
PR

Piet Oudolf
MGC

Chris Overdorf
AMN, SCP

François Paris
WSG

Nilesh Patel
GFB

Bertrand Paulet
MOR

Brian Pavlovec
CHS

Renzo Piano
AIC

Emily Pizzuto
NEP

Jim Polshek
AMN

Wah Poon
PDM

Neil Porter
CRY, GFB, NBW, PDM,
POT, SCG, TCL, WPA

James Poulson
SCP

Gérard Pras
ESS, EVR, GOL

Gerardo Puente
GFB

Jenna Rauscher
GGN office

Steve Ray
AMN, SCP

Mark Reddington
MOM

Peter Rice
VIS

Martin Richman
SCG

Ian Ritchie
EDF, TER, VIS

Jose Rosa
GFB, PDM

Claudia Ruitenberg
WPA

Cass Salzwedel
GGN office, MN

Paul Schell
CHS

Todd Schliemann
AMN

Jim Schmidt
AMN

Leni Schwendinger
MOM

Anton Segerstrom
SCP

Henry Segerstrom
SCP

Simon Skeffington
GP

John Smart
SCG

Pierre Solbes
MAR

Kinna Stallard
SCG, GP office, MN

Peter Steinbrueck
CHS

Charles Stirton
NBW

Robbie Stoakes
CRY

Ivor Stokes
NBW

Barbara Swift
CHS

Jim Takamune
SCP

Mieke Tanghe
WPA, TCL

Brad Tong
CHS

Edward Uhlir
MGC

Evert Verhagen
WPA

Rene Vilijn
WPA

Shelagh Wakely
PDM

Julia Wessendorf
TCL, GFB, PDM

Marcia West
CHS, MOM, NEP, PR

Pauline Wieringa
WPA

Guillermo Wieland
VIS

Peter B. Willberg
Designer of *Moving Horizons*

Grant Wilson
SCP

Rick Zeive
CHS

Illustration Credits

Acknowledgements

The majority of projects in this book are complex; this type of work is not done by one lone designer but by teams of people. I would like to express my gratitude and appreciation to everyone that has made these projects into a reality. The collective talent, energy, passion and compassion have been and continue to be an amazement and a driving force.

I would like to expressly acknowledge my close working partners from over the years: Sylvie Farges in Paris, Neil Porter and Mary Bowman in London, and Jennifer Guthrie and Shannon Nichol in Seattle. Their skills and dedication continue to foster the work of landscape architecture.

I want to thank Birkhäuser – Publishers for Architecture for their support and commitment to the creation of this book. In particular Andreas Müller, our editor, who worked tirelessly with the unique virtue of consistent, humored diplomacy. I also wish to thank the author Jane Amidon who not only embraced this monumental task, but wrote with such clarity and grace. Thanks would not be complete without Peter Willberg, whose graphic design abilities translated the essence of the work to the book, and Aaron Betsky, whom I respect as one of the foremost experts and intellectuals in today's architecture world.

A book takes many resources to compile; ours with its disparate locations and languages was daunting. I wish to express my gratitude to the people that helped sponsor this book with Birkhäuser. Deepest appreciation to Henry and Elizabeth Segerstrom, Victoria Reed, and Marc Chacon and Geoffrey Milspaw of Associated Imports.

In the process of bringing together information on projects that span three offices and nearly three decades, every attempt has been made to accurately credit the contributions of hundreds of people (please see photo album in appendix). In the event that a name has been overlooked, the omission is inadvertent. The quality of professionalism and personal energy offered by each colleague, client and collaborator has shaped the work seen in these pages and will continue to play a defining role in the practices of Gustafson Porter and Gustafson Guthrie Nichol.

Kathryn Gustafson December 2004